With all our love this weekend
as your going to school.
    Love Mom & Dad
      "143"

Emily Dickinson's
Gardens

*A celebration of a poet
and gardener*

Marta McDowell

McGraw·Hill

New York   Chicago   San Francisco   Lisbon   London   Madrid   Mexico City
Milan   New Delhi   San Juan   Seoul   Singapore   Sydney   Toronto

The *McGraw·Hill* Companies

Library of Congress Cataloging-in-Publication Data

McDowell, Marta.
    Emily Dickinson's gardens : a celebration of a poet and gardener / Marta McDowell.
        p.   cm.
    Includes bibliographical references and index.
    ISBN 0-07-142409-1 (hardcover)
        1. Dickinson, Emily, 1830–1886—Knowledge—Gardening.   2. Poets, American—
Homes and haunts—Massachusetts—Amherst.   3. Dickinson, Emily, 1830–1886—
Knowledge—Botany.   4. Gardening—Massachusetts—Amherst.   5. Gardens in literature.
6. Flowers in literature.   7. Botany in literature.   I. Title.

    PS1541.Z5M217   2005
    811'.4—dc22   2004009442

Permission to reprint literary selections and artwork can be found on pages 207–208, which are to be considered an extension of this copyright page.

1 2 3 4 5 6 7 8 9 0   FGR/FGR   3 2 1 0 9 8 7 6 5 4

ISBN 0-07-142409-1

Interior design by Monica Baziuk

McGraw-Hill books are available at special quantity discounts to use as premiums and sales promotions, or for use in corporate training programs. For more information, please write to the Director of Special Sales, Professional Publishing, McGraw-Hill, Two Penn Plaza, New York, NY 10121-2298. Or contact your local bookstore.

This book is printed on acid-free paper.

CONTENTS

❖

❖

1

EARLY SPRING

2

LATE SPRING

3

EARLY SUMMER

4

LATE SUMMER

5

AUTUMN

6

WINTER

❖

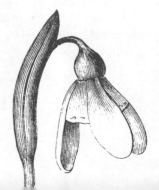

ACKNOWLEDGMENTS

*F*or an idea growing into a book, I have many people to thank. I am in debt to Cindy Dickinson, the curator of the Homestead, who conducted my first tour of the Homestead and whose nametag at the time read "No relation." She has answered innumerable questions and clarified so many facts. I am humbled by her graciousness and her encyclopedic knowledge. Ed Davis, professor emeritus of botany at the University of Massachusetts–Amherst, thank you for the impromptu lessons on botany and the history of botany in the nineteenth century. The librarians in Special Collections at the Jones Library in Amherst, the Houghton Library at Harvard College, the New York Botanical Garden, the Massachusetts Horticultural Society, the Brown University Library, the Horticultural Society of New York, and the Frost Library at Amherst College should receive special bonuses for patience and thoroughness.

Jenny Bent, agent extraordinaire and most special niece, your standards and encouragement were equally high. My editor, Meg Leder, saw the possibilities and delivered them. Jane Davenport, Linda O'Gorman, and Sandra Swan were the readers who always wanted it to be better. Sarah Stanley, your eyes, organization, and ministrations brought the images together in spite of last-minute technical difficulties.

Special thanks to my colleagues at Reeves-Reed Arboretum, who picked up the slack in the borders while I was out. To my dear family, who instilled a love of books and words. And to my husband, Kirke, without whom this seed would never have germinated.

INTRODUCTION

$\mathcal{E}$mily Dickinson was a gardener.

It is a little-known fact. You can host an Emily Dickinson game show with your friends. Say her name, and ask them what they think of first. It may be a white dress—or poetry, of course—or a well-known image of a sixteen-year-old girl staring boldly out of a daguerreotype. It probably won't be gardening.

Emily Dickinson as a gardener doesn't fit with the Emily Dickinson mythology. The myths were based on the real phobias of her later years but were also stoked by her first editor, Mabel Loomis Todd, to promote book sales. Since her death in 1886, she has been psychoanalyzed, compared to medieval cloistered mystics, and called "the madwoman in the attic." All she lacked was a turret.

But beyond being the stuff of legend, she was also a real person devoted to her family, with pleasures and pastimes and friends who were important to her. She shared a love of plants with her parents and siblings. To friends, she sent bouquets, and to her numerous correspondents—over 1,000 of her letters have been found—she often enclosed flowers to punctuate a message. She collected wildflowers, walking with her dog, Carlo. She studied botany at Amherst Academy. She grew houseplants and tended a glassed conservatory off her father's

Emily Dickinson at sixteen. Note the flowers in her hand and the book on the table. From the Amherst College Archives and Special Collections.

study. In winter she forced hyacinth bulbs and in summer she knelt on a red blanket in her flower borders, performing horticulture's familiar rituals.

I hope that Emily will forgive me if I use her Christian name. Not having been properly introduced, I should call her Miss Dickinson. But in reading her poems and letters, in sifting out garden references, I feel that I've gotten to know her, and I hope you will get to know her too.

A word about spelling, grammar, and punctuation. It is, to our best knowledge, Emily's own. The poems and quotes from letters that you'll read in this volume are taken from the latest editions by two Harvard scholars: Ralph W. Franklin and Thomas H. Johnson. Their careful deciphering of manuscripts led them to use her original words, transcribed directly from her pen. So if the punctuation is peculiar or the spelling unusual, know that it was as she wrote it, with one exception. I've taken the liberty of relocating a few jarring apostrophes, for example, changing "is'nt" to "isn't."

One final note: Emily didn't title her poems. In this book, the number in parentheses below each poem indicates the chronological order assigned to it in Ralph Franklin's edition of her poems.

This book is arranged in calendar fashion, following the seasons. Welcome to Emily Dickinson's gardening year.

Answer July
Where is the Bee -
Where is the Blush -
Where is the Hay?

Ah, said July -
Where is the Seed -
Where is the Bud -
Where is the May -
Answer Thee - me -

Nay - said the May -
Show me the Snow -
Show me the Bells -
Show me the Jay!

Quibbled the Jay -
Where be the Maize -
Where be the Haze -
Where be the Bur?
Here - said the Year -

(667)

EARLY SPRING

Emily Dickinson's Garden

*I*f you stand in front of the Homestead in Amherst, you can use your imagination, what Emily called "reverie," to summon up the landscape as she knew it in the mid-1800s.

Main Street is an unpaved road. Today's sidewalks, telephone poles, and fire hydrants disappear, as do the signs that announce this house and its neighbor as destinations for tourists and literary pilgrims. Traffic noise vanishes, to be replaced by the occasional clomp of hooves and click of tack.

The front yard is separated from Main Street by a double line, a hedge of clipped, evergreen hemlocks and a stylish fence of square pickets. From the ornate front gate, some steps above the ruts of the half-frozen street, you look south over an acreage of stubble which in summer earned the name "the Dickinson meadow." Dark arms and trunks of shade trees stood sentinel near the stoop; chestnuts, oaks, and other denizens of the northeastern deciduous forest cast shadows on the lawn.

The Dickinson Homestead circa 1870

Looking toward the brick house, the carriage driveway curved around it from the right, or west, side. If you walked up the drive, at some distance from the house was a grove of trees sheltering it from the hot winds of summer and blocking some of the Arctic blasts which came crashing down from Canada in winter. In later years, Emily's father built a house next door for Austin and his new bride, Susan ("Sister Sue" to Emily). A path between the houses wound among the trees. Emily could look out her bedroom window along the path and see her niece, nephews, and the neighborhood children playing in the yard. Susan's hollyhocks edged the path.

Past the path, a large carriage house and barn occupied the rear of the property, shaded by large oak trees. Two horses and numerous cows, chickens, and pigs occupied it, providing the households with transportation, milk, and meat. Along the barn, Emily's mother grew her prizewinning figs. Grapes trellised on the side of the barn looked over the fruit trees, apples, pears, and cherries that grew down the slope.

Continuing past the barn, you would finally see Emily's garden on the east side of the house. A path of flagstones, local granite, led down a mild incline through the lawn, alongside the fruit trees and flower beds. Lily of the valley carpeted some beds, perfuming the spring pansies. Honeysuckle sweetened the air from a trellis. Hedges of peonies lent their massive display to May. Roses, awaiting their June cue, clambered over a summer house. Masses of spring bulbs—hyacinths and daffodils—were followed by a profusion of annuals and perennials: sweet peas, nasturtiums, lilies, and marigolds, to name a few. Emily's niece Mattie described it as "a meandering mass of bloom."[1]

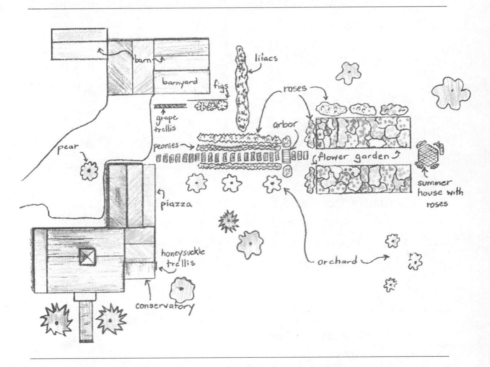

Emily's garden, based on her descriptions and the recollections of her friends and family

A piazza overlooked the west side of the property, just outside the parlor; glass doors opened on to it. Today we would call it a deck, but then the style was Italian and romantic, so *piazza* was the word. Potted plants like oleander and pomegranate, which would not have survived outside in a Massachusetts winter, blossomed there in summer. Emily and her sister, Vinnie, sat on the piazza in fine weather. They enjoyed the ultimate gardener's reward—those moments of surveying one's handiwork after the hard work is done.

A Gardener's Home and a Gardening Family

Amherst, Massachusetts, was the backdrop for Emily Dickinson's garden. Known today as a college town, it was originally an extension of the Puritan settlements on the coast. Farmers and fur traders followed on the heels of the first colonists, exploring the broad Connecticut River and its banks. They founded Amherst in 1745, a small town nestled in what is aptly called the Pioneer Valley. Emily once told her brother that Amherst "seems indeed to be a bit of Eden."

Plants flourish here, in addition to poets. Amherst lies on a fertile spur of land due east of the Connecticut River, eighty miles inland from Boston. When Emily lived in Amherst, it was a landscape of hills, wildflowers, and fields.

The fields were farmed. Emily's Amherst was a market town; many of her neighbors were farmers. Everyone had an orchard and vegetable garden to enrich the summer table and the winter pantry. In Emily's first published poem, a valentine, she wrote:

જ્

**Put down the apple Adam
And come away with me
So shal't thou have a pippin
From off my Father's tree!**

(2A)

Her father's first apple trees were at the Dickinson Homestead, an imposing brick house perched on a knoll at 280 Main Street, just a short walk from the center of town.

Built in proper Federal style in 1813 by Emily's grandfather, Samuel Fowler Dickinson, it was the axis of Emily's world. She was born at the Homestead, gardened there for forty of her fifty-five years, and died there. It temporarily passed out of the Dickinson family after her grandfather went bankrupt, overextending his credit in establishing a new school, Amherst College, that was his obsession. During the hiatus, Emily and her family set up housekeeping in a clapboard house on North Pleasant Street when she was nine years old. The Pleasant Street house was demolished in the 1920s.

Emily's father, Edward, a prominent Amherst attorney like his father and the treasurer of Amherst College, reacquired the Dickinson Homestead in the 1850s. The property included two and a half acres surrounding the house and barn and an eleven-acre meadow across the road. Edward planted trees on his property, and was especially interested in the kitchen garden. "The strawberries are abundant here," he

Edward Dickinson, Emily's father, and Emily Norcross Dickinson, Emily's mother

wrote to Emily Norcross, his future wife, "& cherries & currants are nearly ripe. The whole vegetable kingdom now appears in its greatest beauty." [2] He also did some of the legwork for his daughter's garden. "Tell . . . papa to come with the sweet-williams," Emily ordered in 1859. [3]

Her mother, Emily Norcross Dickinson, was also a gardener. Her daughter described her as busy, "with fruit, and plants, and chickens, and sympathizing friends, she really was so hurried she hardly knew what to do." [4] A fine cook and homemaker, she decorated with her

Emily, Austin, and Lavinia at ages nine, ten, and seven

flower garden, cutting stems and arranging them in pitchers around the house. She gave her children a love of horticulture. Emily once said, "I was reared in the garden, you know."⁵

Emily, the middle child, was born in 1830. She followed a year after Austin; in 1833 Lavinia, the youngest, was born. This trio—Emily, Austin, and Vinnie, as she was called—shared a passion for plants, a tight-knit relationship, and a lifelong occupancy of the Dickinson property.

Austin, like their father, was a great planter of trees. As a teenager, he planted a conifer grove near their house. Emily wrote to her brother, "We all went down this morning and the trees look beautifully. Every one is growing, and when the west wind blows, the pines lift their light leaves and make sweet music."⁶

Vinnie was Emily's lifelong companion. She was also a gardener: Emily describes her making borders and training vines. And she wasn't afraid to dig—Emily refers to her "subsoiling" in the garden.

In an early portrait with her siblings, Emily is nine years old, shown with red hair and a gentle smile. Though the three look stilted, in later years Emily must have appreciated that the artist showed her holding a book and white rose: the written word and a flower. In the Victorian language of flowers, the white rose was the symbol of purity and of silence, virtues wished for children of the time. Little did the artist know that Emily Dickinson's voice would prove perennial.

Early Spring in Emily Dickinson's Garden

"*There* is no more snow"!
(30)

The vernal equinox is just past. While an occasional nor'easter still roars up the Atlantic coast, dumping snow in central New England, it is spring snow and short-lived. One March day, Emily notes, "Mother went rambling, and came in with a burdock on her shawl, so we know that the snow has perished from the earth. Noah would have liked mother." [7]

In Emily's garden, the buds begin to swell on the branches of the cherry trees, jutting their elbows into the lengthening and warmer days. As the ground thaws, the lawn gets greener and bare paths turn to mud. Plants wake up. Songbirds charm the trees. Emily called March "that month of proclamation." [8]

A Little Catalogue of Emily's Early Spring Flowers

SNOWDROP (*Galanthus nivalis*) The first flowers to bloom in Emily's garden are the little bulbs. Heralds of spring, the snowdrops lead the way; their nodding, bell-shaped flowers are their own proclamation. They are sweet-smelling and long-lived. As an added bonus, snowdrops increase every year, carpeting an area with white.

New feet within my garden go -
New fingers stir the sod -
A Troubadour opon the Elm
Betrays the solitude.

New Children play opon the green -
New Weary sleep below -
And still the pensive Spring returns -
And still the punctual snow!

(79)

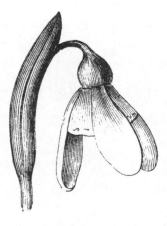

Snowdrop

⇥| TIP |⇤

Crocuses grow from small corms, underground stems crowned by a growing bud. When you select the corms, make sure they are firm to the touch. It's like picking out an onion. In autumn, plant them three to four inches deep in a sunny spot with well-drained soil. Thin, grass-like leaves will appear first in early spring; then the flowers will push straight up like soldiers. Emily dubbed them "martial." The foliage will die down before summer. Leave the foliage to die completely, rather than cutting it. The green leaves are photosynthesizing, building up food reserves for the next bloom.

CROCUS (*Crocus spp.*) In one of her poems, Emily called crocus the "Vassal of the snow." [9] A member of the iris family, a crocus has a cup-shaped flower. Tradition dedicates it to St. Valentine since it blooms near his day.

The "Cloth of Gold" crocus has been cultivated since 1587. Other heirloom crocuses that Emily might have grown in her garden are the "Tommies," *Crocus tommasinianus*, pale to deep lilac with a white heart. Introduced in the nursery trade in 1847, Tommies are also the most rodent-resistant crocus; the species unfortunately is a favorite of chipmunks.

TULIP (*Tulipa spp.*) During this time, the tulips start to push up, their pointed green

Crocus

tips emerging like spires through the layers of brown leaves. One of her earliest poems, a sort of schoolgirl riddle, describes a tulip:

> She slept beneath a tree -
> Remembered but by me.
> I touched her Cradle mute -
> She recognized the foot -
> Put on her Carmine suit
> And see!
>
> (15)

Hyacinth

Hyacinth (*Hyacinth orientalis*) Dense hyacinth buds surface in her garden this time of year, building up fragrance for their mid-spring bloom. Gardeners often tell time by the bloom season rather than the calendar, and Emily remembered a glance from a friend "in Hyacinth time." In a thank-you note Emily once wrote, "The Snow will guide the Hyacinths to where their Mates are sleeping, in Vinnie's sainted Garden."[10] Vinnie no doubt planted them for her.

Pansy (*Viola tricolor*) Another spring flower that carpets Emily's garden is the pansy. Pansies are called Johnny-jump-ups for their tendency to spread around the garden. Their charming faces pop up in unlikely places. Pansies are edible, so they make lovely additions to salads and superb decorations for ice molds or cakes. When Emily baked gingerbread, she used them to decorate the flat shiny tops. Like many flowers of the season, they are diminutive.

A pansy is particular only about the weather. To one friend, Emily wrote, "That a pansy is transitive, is its only pang."[11] It will grow in cold weather, languish in hot.

⇥ BULBS ⇤

Bulbs fascinated Emily, but she had a gardener's patience. They are not for you if you're looking for instant gratification; once you're done with the hard work of burying them underground in the fall, all you've got is anticipation as the bulbs lie dormant, without a hint of green.

Each bulb is a collection of ghostly, immature leaves held together at the base where roots emerge. The roots anchor the bulb, collect water, and soak up minerals to carry it through the winter. Bulbs are actually a mass of stored food, fistfuls of energy that will push up leaves and flowers.

In Emily's garden, bulbs are mixed with other plants so that when their show is over, the dull but necessary foliage is hidden by something that will bloom later. Do this in your own garden too.

The word "pansy" comes from the French word that means "to think." Thus a pansy is pensive, with its flowers that look like faces, faces that invite contemplation. Perhaps that is why another nickname for this flower is "heart's-ease." Emily gathered pansies into her bouquets and sent them to friends with accompanying rhyme.

I'm the little "Heart's Ease"!
I don't care for pouting skies!
If the Butterfly delay
Can I, therefore, stay away?

Heart's-ease or pansy

If the Coward Bumble Bee
In his chimney corner stay,
I, must resoluter be!
Who'll apologize for me?

Dear - Old fashioned, little flower!
Eden is old fashioned, too!
Birds are antiquated fellows!
Heaven does not change her blue.
Nor will I, the little Heart's Ease -
Ever be induced to do!

   (167)

PEONY (*Paeonia spp.*) As spring moves forward, the earth warms and more perennials break, shouldering buds up through the soil. One of the plants breaking ground in Emily's garden is the peony, actually masses of peonies. Mattie described "ribbons of peony hedges"[12] that edged the garden. In one of Emily's early letters, she compares the first tips to the nose of the son of the stable hand. "Tell Vinnie I counted three peony noses, red as Sammie Matthew's, just out of the ground."[13] Peonies, unlike most herbaceous plants, surface with buds of deep burgundy.

PUSSYWILLOW (*Salix discolor*) When Emily sent flowers to her friends, one early spring choice was a branch of pussywillow, sent with an enclosure that said, "Nature's buff message - left for you in Amherst. She had not time to call. You see her Father and my Father were brothers."[14] The buff-colored pussywillow buds emerge in late February like the soft, fuzzy toes of one of Vinnie's kittens. Appropriate that the flowers are called catkins.

Dense, clustering pussywillow shrubs grew wild in swampy, sunny places around Amherst. They are easy to domesticate. Emily may have cut a branch on one of her many explorations, rooted it in water, and planted it in the garden herself. Left out of water, her cut branches dried perfectly, preserving their furry buds indefinitely.

BLUEBELL (*Mertensia virginica*) Emily liked to include pressed flowers in her letters. In one brief note to fellow poet Helen Hunt Jackson, she sent bluebells. "Bluebell" is a common name that graces several plants, including a bulb, English bluebells or *Hyacinthoides non-scripta*, and a spring ephemeral, Virginia bluebells or *Mertensia virginica*. Because the letter is dated early April, it is most likely the latter, since English bluebells bloom in Amherst in May.

In moist, shady areas of Emily's garden, Virginia bluebells colonize, making outposts when they are left undisturbed. They would have appealed to Emily, unfurling their bright sea-green leaves in March, nodding with blue clusters of blooms in April, sowing their seed and then disappearing by mid-summer. Like her poems, bluebells are startling but succinct.

With the ground warming, the little bulbs spent, and the perennials coming into leaf, the stage is set for the peak spring display in Emily's garden. It is a quiet time of year.

An Early Spring Garden Primer

Early spring is a special time for gardeners because, frankly, there isn't much to do other than watch for new growth. One exception is pruning. Since most woody plants are dormant, it is a good time to shape them up, especially the roses. Early spring is an awkward time for roses; their worst features are exaggerated. Their thorns, which a proper botanist calls "prickles," are prominent. Their canes, the round, straight branches, are skeletal and gangly. But if they look a bit bedraggled, maybe it's because they are ready for a haircut.

How to Prune Old Garden Roses

Emily's garden was full of old garden roses. Most of these varieties bloom only once, in June. Twentieth-century hybrid teas and floribunda roses are "repeat bloomers," often bearing roses into fall, but they sacrifice fragrance and a certain gracefulness for ongoing color displays. This pruning lesson will address old roses rather than their newer— some would say gaudier—cousins.

Before you begin pruning old roses, find your gloves. Gloves should be leather and, if your budget permits, gauntlet style, extending up to the elbows. Wear long pants, a long-sleeved shirt, and a baseball cap. Since you'll be reaching in and around spiky plants, a bit of protective clothing can prevent punctures.

You'll need three tools:

1. A hand pruner, also known as a secateur. For the cleanest cut, use bypass pruners whose blades cross like a scissors, rather than squeeze like a vise. My favorites are Felco brand, with a comfortable red grip. A small diamond sharpener fits the blade to keep it honed to a sharp edge.

Secateur with bypass blades

2. Lopping shears. For canes that are more than half an inch in diameter, you will need more leverage to cut cleanly. Lopping shears look like an enlarged version of hand pruners, with longer handles.

3. A pruning saw. Some canes grow to be more than an inch thick. To remove these venerable canes, you will need the big guns—namely a saw. A pruning saw has a straight grip and blade, as opposed to a bow saw, which has an arching handle. This straight aspect gives you the most access for pruning.

Old garden roses have main canes which grow out of a woody base or directly out of the ground. Depending on the variety, these canes often have side growth, smaller branches that grow out of the canes.

Pruning them is simple. Your goal is to remove all growth that is dead, diseased, or deranged. First, remove the gray, dead canes by cutting them to the base of the plant or the ground, whichever you get to first. By early spring it will be obvious which to remove, since viable canes flush with the green of a new growing season. Also remove any dead side branches that are growing out of live canes. Next, take out any damaged or diseased canes or side growth. Canes that are bent from snow or winter wind won't recover. Disease, like rose canker, shows up as vertical scars along the canes. Insects, like rose borers, drill small round holes. Be tough. It is better for the plant if you take out any weakened growth.

After removing dead and diseased growth, you've reached the aesthetic step: lightly shape the rose by removing canes that detract from the beauty of the plant. This might mean taking off a cane that grows in the wrong direction. It might mean removing extra canes that make the plant too wide. With old garden roses, you sacrifice the bloom on anything you cut off in early spring; so when in doubt, leave it and prune after the flush of flowers in June.

Depending on the plant, and on your personality, you may be left with a much smaller plant. Fear not, the growing season is upon us.

LATE SPRING

The Education of a Gardener

Spring in Amherst is euphoric, a visual and olfactory high. Emily called spring an inundation. Bright green leaves pick up the wind, mimicking the sound a stream makes riffling over rocks. The sun heats up blossoms, drawing out their scent. "Today is very beautiful -" Emily once wrote to Austin, "just as bright, just as blue, just as green and as white, and as crimson, as the cherry trees full in bloom, and the half opening peach blossoms, and the grass just waving, and sky and hill and cloud, can make it, if they try." [1]

For her first nine years, Emily encountered spring outside the doors of the old Dickinson Homestead. In 1840, however, Emily and her family moved to a house on North Pleasant Street, a few blocks from where she was born. Emily had new ground to garden.

We don't know much about the North Pleasant Street garden. The only surviving picture shows a comfortable white clapboard house with a large porch that looks out on fruit trees in the front yard. Emily wrote to Austin in the spring, "Our trees are all very full of blossoms now and - they look very handsome." [2]

When the girls' ages hit double digits, their father sent Emily and Vinnie to Amherst Academy, what we would think of as high school. The Academy taught Emily her first formal lessons on plants. She described her studies enthusiastically (and without punctuation) to her friend Jane Humphrey: "... besides Latin I study History and Botany I like the school very much indeed." She adds, "My Plants grow beautifully." [3]

Amherst Academy also afforded her an unusual educational opportunity, especially given the period. Edward Hitchcock, the president of Amherst College, and his colleagues lectured on natural history topics like botany and geology. Boys and girls from Amherst Academy attended these classes on a regular basis. "We found that the admission of girls to such lectures as they could understand," one writer documented in 1835, "was a practice of some years' standing, and ... no evil had been found to result from it." [4] In addition to his lectures, Dr. Hitchcock also preached at Sunday services and authored books. "When Flowers annually died, and I was a child," Emily remembered, "I used to read Dr. Hitchcock's Book on the Flowers of North America. This comforted their Absence - assuring me they lived." [5]

In addition to Dr. Hitchcock and his books, Amherst Academy introduced Emily to other books on flowers, including Almira Lincoln's textbook *Familiar Lectures on Botany*, a hugely popular book that went through nine editions in ten years.

The study of plants and flowers was considered a genteel occupation for women. Open the little brown book that Emily opened, and read the introduction from Mrs. Lincoln: "The study of Botany seems peculiarly adapted to females; the objects of its investigation are beautiful and delicate; its pursuit leading to exercise in the open air is conducive to health and cheerfulness." [6]

Botany was the rage for theological reasons as well. During those decades of evangelical Protestantism in Amherst, studying natural phenomena was considered an avenue to understanding the plan of the Deity. A popular saying was "His pencil grows in every flower." [7]

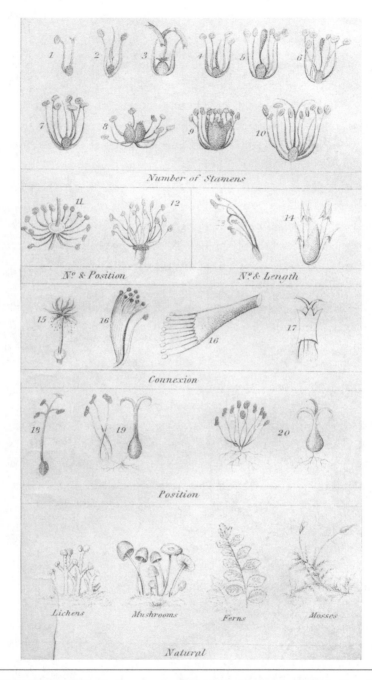

When Emily studied botany, one of the books she used was Mrs. Lincoln's.

The Herbarium

While studying botany, Emily collected flowers and created a herbarium, a collection of pressed, dried plants organized systematically. It was a popular hobby in those days, part of a nineteenth-century craving to make scrapbooks and photograph albums. "I have been to walk to-night," Emily wrote her friend Abiah Root, "and got some very choice wild flowers. I wish you had some of them.... I am going to send you a little geranium leaf in this letter, which you must press for me. Have you made an herbarium yet? I hope you will if you have not, it would be such a treasure to you; most all the girls are making one. If you do, perhaps I can make some additions to it from flowers growing around here." [8]

Emily's sixty-six-page herbarium is beautifully arranged, bound in leather with a green fabric cover embossed in a floral pattern. It looks like an expensive photo album. And its binding was a status symbol. Many girls making herbaria would have used single sheets put together "loose leaf" in a portfolio, a simpler and cheaper way to collect dried plants.

Emily collected a specimen of each plant, over four hundred of them, then pressed and dried them in between sheets of blotting paper. It's likely that she had a plant press to go along with the herbarium. A press is made of two rectangular pieces of wood or an assembled wood lath with heavy straps to tie it together tightly. Otherwise she would have dried her plants in the pages of large books. Emily laid out the dried plants, not exactly like a collage, but as a graphic designer might. Each specimen is carefully mounted with strips of gummed paper and neatly labeled in her best penmanship.

The layouts are lovely; on many pages Emily offset a single large specimen with several smaller ones. Sometimes the arrangements are whimsical, two daisies crisscrossed at the bottom of a page like swords supporting a coat of arms. Others are vigorous, three stems of aralia fanned out over a tripartite leaf of hepatica. Later in the album, Emily inserted more specimens per page, as if she worried about running out of room. All the pages in the album are used. As she continued to collect specimens, she had to fit them in wherever she found space.

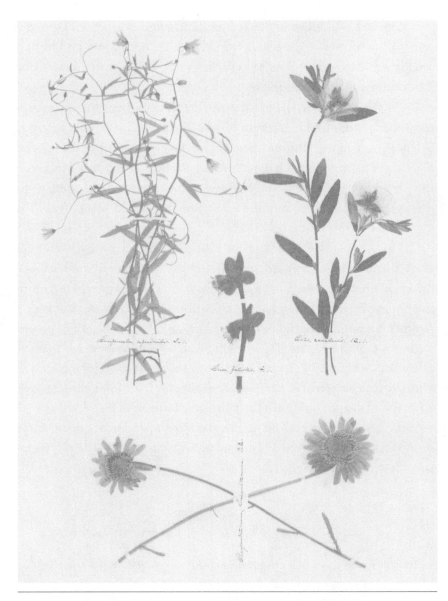

On the eighth page of the herbarium she grouped three wildflowers: marsh bellflower (*Campanula aparinoides*), leatherwood (*Dirca palustris*), and frostweed (*Cistus candensis*). She added a flower grown in the garden and the meadow, ox-eyed daisy (*Chrysanthemum leucanthemum*). She wrote numbers below each name to indicate the class and order, determined by counting the stamens and pistils, respectively, of the flower.

She was catholic in her collecting. She included vegetables (potato, tomato, cucumber) and trees (horse chestnut, tulip, dogwood). She cast a wide net across the plant kingdom, even catching two algae—one freshwater and one from the sea.

As she assembled the herbarium, Emily tested different methods for putting order to the diversity. Most often pages are artistic with different genera mixed. But on a few pages, she grouped all of the species of one genus together: a page of violas, another of narcissus. Seasons mingle. Flowers of lobelia and dogtooth violet bloom on the same page, even though they open months apart. She integrated plants from the garden and plants from the wild.

For a detective in search of Emily's garden, the herbarium is stuffed with clues. The garden flowers that made the cut are hard evidence of what she grew, or at least knew of. One of her poems mentions the poppy; her herbarium has both California poppy (*Eschscholzia californica*) and opium poppy (*Papaver somniferum*).[9] From one of her poems we know that "The Lilac is an ancient Shrub,"[10] and now we see that she grew late-blooming Persian lilac (*Syringa persica*) as well as common lilac (*Syringa vulgaris*). She left us a visual plant list of her garden beds: zinnias and snapdragons, nasturtiums and four-o'clocks.

Emily wrote the name of the plant with proper botanical Latin nomenclature: the *genus*, or generic name, followed by the *species*, or specific epithet.

⇥ WHAT'S IN A NAME? ⇤

When Emily gave her collection captions, she was using a system invented by Swedish naturalist Carolus Linnaeus (a.k.a. Carl von Linne) a century before her. The study of plants, like any other discipline, has its own vocabulary. But botany and horticulture also have their own language: botanical Latin. In 1753, when Linnaeus published *continued* —————————————————————————————————

his *Species Plantarum,* he brought order out of chaos for the world of naming plants. His two-part naming system, binomial nomenclature, is like a phone book for plants.

The plant names in Emily's herbarium divide into two easy parts, genus and species, just as a phone number is made up of area code plus exchange and a unique phone number. A simple cheat sheet goes as follows:

❖ **On genus.** The general group or broad category of plants. I remember "genus is generic; species is specific." As in this book, you'll see that the genus is italic and capitalized. The plural of genus is "genera."

❖ **On species.** The specific characteristics of a plant. Within the genus, the species or, if you want to get technical, "specific epithet," describes a plant that reproduces with identifiable traits. (Note that the abbreviation for the plural of species is "spp.")

❖ **On variety.** In flower catalogues of Emily's day, a new type of category emerged: the variety. A salute to capitalism, a variety has distinguishing traits within a species that make it marketable in the nurseries. Horticultural varieties come in two flavors. Cultivars, or *culti*vated *vari*eties, are man-made, created in a greenhouse or garden by cross-pollinating two individual plants. Think of it as unnatural selection. The other kind of variety is called a sport, or sport of nature. Sports, truth be told, are mutations. They are discovered by a gardener or plant collector in a garden or in the wild and then propagated.

If you're serious about gardening, it's time to brush up on your botanical Latin. It's the only way you'll know for sure what you're planning and planting.

"I Was Always Attached to Mud"

Emily's herbarium lets us accompany her on her wildflower excursions, whispering hints of the habitats that she encountered. You'll have to wade into the tall grass to join her in collecting butterfly weed and goldenrod from the meadow. And some of the plants are postcards from the edge, peering out from the edge of the forest canopy. Mountain laurel and elderberry thrive in the combination of rich soil and partial shade, making an understory for the trees.

In addition to a walk in the woods, I hope you don't mind the mud. Wandering in the streams around her home, Emily would often come home dirty and bedraggled. In later years, she wrote, "Two things I have lost with Childhood, the rapture of losing my shoe in the mud and going Home barefoot, wading for Cardinal flowers and the mother's reproof which was more for my sake than her weary own for she frowned with a smile." [11] There was a stream that ran through the Dickinson meadow, and other streams, now flowing underground in Amherst culverts, ready for wading. Deep red cardinal flowers bloomed in moist soils. Well into adulthood, Emily wrote, "I was always attached to Mud." [12]

Emily had a propensity for solitary wildflower walks, and this tendency did not go unnoticed by her family. In one of Emily's letters, you can hear her mother's voice, telling her to be careful in a hundred little ways, and her older brother's teasing. "When much in the Woods as a little Girl, I was told that the Snake would bite me, that I might pick a poisonous flower, or Goblins kidnap me, but I went along and met no one but Angels, who were far shyer of me, than I could be of them, so I hav'nt that confidence in fraud which many exercise." [13]

Her father took a different approach to solving the problem of Emily's solo flights. He bought her a really big dog. She named him Carlo, after a canine that appeared in a favorite novel entitled *Reveries of a Bachelor*, and called him her "Shaggy Ally." [14] Describing her companions to a new correspondent, she listed, "Hills - Sir - and the Sundown - and a Dog - large as myself, that my Father bought me - They are better than Beings - because they know - but do not tell." [15]

For Emily, there was nothing like a dog to take on wildflower walks: "Could'nt Carlo, and you and I walk in the meadows an hour - and nobody care but the Bobolink, and his - a silver scruple?" [16]

Carlo also made an excellent gardening supervisor.

Within my Garden, rides a Bird
Opon a single Wheel -
Whose spokes a dizzy music make
As 'twere a travelling Mill -

He never stops, but slackens
Above the Ripest Rose -
Partakes without alighting
And praises as he goes,

Till every spice is tasted -
And then his Fairy Gig
Reels in remoter atmospheres -
And I rejoin my Dog,

And He and I, perplex us
If positive, 'twere we -
Or bore the Garden in the Brain
This Curiosity -

But He, the best Logician,
Refers my clumsy eye -
To just vibrating Blossoms!
An exquisite Reply!

(370)

"I talk of all these things with Carlo," Emily writes to a friend, "and his eyes grow meaning, and his shaggy feet keep a slower pace . . ." [17] Evidently Carlo didn't have the doggish habit of digging holes in the garden with those shaggy paws, or if he did, Emily didn't mention it.

Carlo lived a long life with Emily; he was her constant companion for sixteen years. One Amherst woman remembered "when, as a little girl, [I] went walking with Miss Dickinson while the huge dog stalked solemnly beside us. 'Gracie,' said Miss Dickinson, 'Do you know that I believe that the first to come and greet me when I go to heaven will be this dear, faithful old friend Carlo?'" [18] When he died, Emily wrote to a friend, "Carlo died. Would you instruct me now?" [19] After he was gone, Emily curtailed her excursions. "I explore but little since my mute Confederate, yet the 'infinite Beauty' of which you speak comes too near to seek." [20] Carlo may have been mute, but he added to the richness of Emily's gardening life.

A Little Catalogue of Emily's Spring Ephemerals

While Emily reveled in her solitary walks and her canine companion, she also explored with her friends. "There were several pleasure parties of which I was a member, and in our rambles we found many and many beautiful children of spring, which I will mention and see if you have found them, - the trailing arbutus, adder's tongue, yellow violets, liverleaf, blood-root, and many other smaller flowers." [21] What a lovely time they must have had on their tramp through the spring woods.

The flowers Emily itemizes are called spring ephemerals because, in the heat of summer, both flower and foliage disappear. The plants go dormant, protecting themselves from the harshness of all of the New England seasons except spring.

These plants will grow happily in your shade garden if you give them a bit of extra attention at the start. They are available from specialty dealers (see the Resources). Create a woodland environment for them, shady and rich with leaf loam; they should create small colonies.

TRAILING ARBUTUS (*Epigaea repens*) The trailing arbutus has oval leaves that shoulder their way up through the leaves on a woodland floor. Its pink or white flowers bloom through May, lending it one of its other common names: mayflower. Rumor has it that the Massachusetts state flower got its name from the Pilgrims, who christened it after their ship. After one New England winter, they must have been happy to see anything bloom. Emily used mayflower to catalogue the spring: "The mud is very deep - up to the wagons' stomachs - arbutus making pink clothes, and everything alive." [22]

Pink - small - and punctual -
Aromatic - low -
Covert in April -
Candid - in May -

Dear to the Moss -
Known of the Knoll -
Next to the Robin
In every Human Soul -

Bold little Beauty -
Bedecked with thee
Nature forswears
Antiquity -

(1357A)

ADDER'S-TONGUE (*Erythronium americanum*) The long, protruding stamen sticking out of the flower suggested this flower's reptilian nickname, *adder's-tongue*. You'll also hear it called trout lily because its speckled leaves reminded someone with a lyrical bent of the scales on that fish. Its flowers are yellow and the petals are recurved. Adder's-tongue colonizes shady woodlands like the ones around Amherst, blooming from March through May. One spring, with a gift of adder's-tongue, Emily enclosed this poem, noting their dappled leaves.

 ⌒

> Their dappled importunity
> Disparage or dismiss -
> The Obloquies of Etiquette
> Are obsolete to Bliss -
>
> (1677)

Emily's poems, including her flower poems, are often opportunities for the dictionary. "Importunity" means *unseasonable*, and May is early for lilies. Cultivated lily bulbs all bloom in the summer. "Obloquies" are slanders, abuses. She implies that bliss beats bad manners. Perhaps Emily's floral acknowledgment was belated, or maybe there was a hidden meaning known only to the recipient.

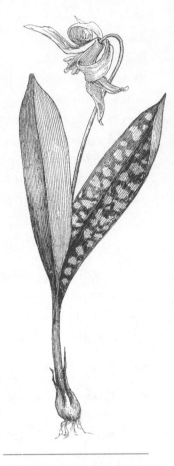

Adder's-tongue showing its "dappled importunity"

YELLOW VIOLETS (*Viola spp.*) *Violet* is the English translation of the Latin name for the flower and the color, though, as Emily saw, not all violets are violet. Her yellow violet was either the round-leafed yellow violet, *Viola rotundifolia*, or the downy yellow violet, *Viola pubescens*.

LIVERLEAF (*Hepatica americana*) The liverleaf's common name sounds a bit medical: *Hepatica* derives from the Greek word for liver, *hepar*. *Hepatitis* comes from the same root word. The lobes of its leaves reminded some ancient pharmacist of the shape of the liver—it's a stretch. At any rate, the name stuck, as did its use as a liver drug. The flowers range from white to pink to purple. Industrious ants help by spreading the ripe seed through the woods where Emily walked.

BLOODROOT (*Sanguinaria canadensis*) Another medical-sounding plant, the bloodroot is named for its red roots and orange sap. The word sounds like *sanguine*, which also means "bloody" or "red in the face." In another of Emily's botany books, great claims are made for this little woodland plant, along with a rather terrifying selection of ailments: "Root highly efficacious in the influenza, hooping-cough, and the late epidemic," the author reports. "Also cathartic, emetic and a . . . stimulant." [23] When Emily found bloodroot with its sweet white blooms in April, she was likely appreciating its aesthetic properties rather than its emetic ones.

Late Spring in Emily Dickinson's Garden

"The lawn is full of south and the odors tangle, and I hear today for the first the river in the tree." [24]

By May in Amherst, the season has gone a bit mad. If there is a warm spell, blossoms seem to open and fade in a day. The colors in the garden are sudden and saturated as if, having gone so long with winter drab and the delicate vernal break, they are taken with their own improbability. Small wonder that gardeners call their reaction "spring fever."

Fruit Trees

The fields and yards of Amherst were full of fruit trees. It was trendy to grow them: apple, plum, cherry, pear, and peach. In a letter to his future wife, Emily's father Edward wrote, "If we had been married this evening, it would have been as pleasant a time as could have been—I found one of our Peach trees in blossom. . . . I always enjoy such pleasant moonlight evenings." [25] Edward, often portrayed as stern, reveals romance in this moonlight stroll in the flowering orchard.

Of Emily's Homestead garden, her niece Mattie tells us, "There were three tall cherry trees in a line, just bordering the flagstone walk at the east side of the house, and all the way down to the garden plum and pear trees, very white and garlandy in spring." [26] Fruit trees bloom enthusiastically and do indeed look like flounces or feather boas.

On the lower terrace in Emily's garden, there was an apple orchard planted in part by her grandfather, Samuel Fowler Dickinson. Orchards at the time were laid out symmetrically, either in a square or in a pattern known as a *quincunx*. If you look at dice, at the faces with five dots, you'll be looking at the layout of a quincunx. Underneath the trees, protesting this inflicted formality, there were long grass and wildflowers, spring violets and buttercups.

The Dickinsons' orchard bloomed in late spring around Whitsunday (known by many as Pentecost), celebrated the seventh Sunday after Easter. Emily often stayed home from church on Sundays with her niece. In honor of the blossoms, Mattie said they joked by calling Whitsunday "White Sunday," since they were "dissenters." [27] Perhaps Emily was sitting in the garden when she wrote this poem:

Some - keep the Sabbath - going to church -
I - keep it - staying at Home -
With a Bobolink - for a Chorister -
And an Orchard - for a Dome -

Some - keep the Sabbath, in Surplice -
I - just wear my wings -
And instead of tolling the bell, for church -
Our little Sexton - sings -

"God" - preaches - a *noted* Clergyman -
And the sermon is never long,
So - instead of getting to Heaven - at last -
I'm - going - all along!

    (236B)

The male bobolink is the image of a clergyman. A bird with black plumage, a yellow nape, and white scapulars, it looks ready to mount the pulpit.

Spring Cleaning

Late spring, the time for a big annual cleanup, is when gardening activities explode. In a letter to Austin, Emily's father once reported, "The wood is piled—the yard cleaned up—grape vines & trees trimmed—garden made & planted, manure got out, potatoes in lot planted, grassland dragged over to loosen the earth & make the grass better. The spring business is about over."[28]

The ground settles, finally wrung of its post-winter thaw, and can be worked. Cultivating breaks up heavy New England soil, giving roots plenty of growing room. Emily knew the value of gardening from the ground up:

Soil of Flint, if steady tilled,
Will refund the Hand -
Seed of Palm, by Lybian Sun
Fructified in Sand -

    (862A)

Steady tilling also allows for soil amendments. Emily's garden had regular additions of well-rotted manure from their stable and barnyard.

Nothing was wasted. The acidic garden soil was "sweetened" with wood ash from the stove or fireplaces and with spent soap suds from the laundry or dishes. Soil has memory, and rewards the gardener who works it wisely.

With the danger of frost in the past, it is time to sow. Over the winter, Emily saved ". . . the seeds in homes of paper until the sun calls them." [29] After the soil was prepared, usually around the end of April, Emily brought out flower seeds that she and Vinnie collected in autumn, received from friends and family, or bought over the winter. A few seeds got special treatment, like the old-fashioned sweet peas, which would have been soaked in water for a few hours before planting to soften the seed hull.

She knelt down and carefully sowed her seeds, covering them in fine garden soil. "I sow my - pageantry / in May - / It rises train by train -" she wrote in one poem,[30] and continues in her spidery handwriting on the same page:

∽—

So build the hillocks gaily -
Thou little spade of mine
Leaving nooks for Daisy
And for Columbine -

(30)

In this poem, Emily talks about sowing in hillocks, raising the soil level for her seeds. She was helping the seedlings along; the raised beds allowed the soil to drain readily. Her "nooks" created a mixed bed rather than ribbon borders. The ribbon pattern, common to Victorian gardens, has parallel single-color strips of annuals. It's the red salvia–blue ageratum–white alyssum combo that still pops up in front yards and outside gas stations today. Emily's was more of a cottage garden, with different kinds of plants mixed together like a crazy quilt.

Spring rains settle the seeds and help them germinate. Rainy days are days of rest for the gardener—quiet, soft days. "It is lonely without the birds today," Emily wrote one May, "for it rains badly, and the little poets have no umbrellas." [31]

Some seeds need to be started inside, and pampered until summer. "Vinnie and Sue, are making Hot Beds - but then the Robins plague them so - they don't accomplish much," Emily wrote one day.[32] A hot bed is a temporary structure for raising seeds and seedlings. Unlike a cold frame, the hot bed is heated, giving seeds and seedlings a toasty space to germinate and grow. It is powered by, of all things, decomposing manure. Emily's sister and sister-in-law were getting the bed ready for transplants.

Late spring is the time to plant late-blooming summer bulbs like lilies and the delicate tubers and bulbs that won't stand the New England climate: dahlias, gladioli, and the like. They are a fantastic menagerie. Lily bulbs look like artichokes, dahlias like some strange fingerling potatoes.

One May, her friend Cornelia Sweetser sent her some bulbs, and Emily replied enthusiastically, "I have long been a Lunatic on Bulbs, though screened by my friends, as Lunacy on any theme is better undivulged. . . . They came in happy safety and rest in their subterranean Home -" [33] The subterranean home of the summer bulbs—all bulbs in fact—should be three times the depth of the bulb itself.

While Emily sows the seeds of summer flowers, the weeds sow themselves. What gardener isn't beset by weeds? Then, as now, dandelions popped up all over lawn and garden. Their serrated leaves lent the dandelion its name, reminding someone French of lion's teeth, or *dent de lion*. The young leaves make a spicy salad or pot green—eating them

Who wouldn't be a lunatic about a bulb like this lily?

seems a fitting punishment for the crime of the deep taproots that they send into the garden. Emily took a different tack, enjoying the dandelion for its images. In different poems, she calls the seedheads "shields" and "millinery." She uses childhood memories of the magic of blowing the seeds.

In a letter, she pressed a dandelion and tied a ribbon around it, enclosing it with a poem. It is a poetic celebration, an ecstatic paean to Spring. Perhaps, instead of broadleaf weed killers, we could memorize Emily's words and broadcast them to our lawns.

The Dandelion's pallid Tube
Astonishes the Grass -
And Winter instantly becomes
An infinite Alas -
The Tube uplifts a signal Bud
And then a shouting Flower -
The Proclamation of the Suns
That sepulture is o'er -

(1565)

The dandelion's "proclamation"

A Little Catalogue of Emily's Late Spring Flowers

May Day is the first of May, a day when Emily and her siblings gathered flowers from the garden to put in May baskets, small containers hung on doors from ribbon handles. Even Austin, when courting, was known to leave a May basket for a special sweetheart. What would have been in bloom?

BLEEDING HEART (*Dicentra spectabilis*) Emily's flower beds boasted this Victorian favorite. Its tall arching stems bear pink hearts that could be drops of blood. Two to three feet high, they are a spectacular spring bloom. Then, romantically, bloom and leaf disappear by mid-summer, inviting comparisons with young love. If you're growing bleeding hearts, be sure to mark their location. It's easy to dig them up by accident.

COLUMBINE (*Aquilegia canadensis*) Columbine is a New England native, with red and yellow flowers bobbing on long stems. It blooms in May in Amherst fields and gardens, sowing its own seeds. The foliage is bluish-green and intricately lobed, like a crocheted edging on old linen.

Columbine is a tolerant sort; it puts up with drought and considerable shade. Its self-seeding often results in color changes in the flowers, so if you want true color, plant fresh seed in late summer or early fall. Transplant it when the seedlings are small—its long taproot makes it a bit finicky about relocating.

For the romantics in the crowd, columbine has a string of common names such as "dancing fairies" and "Harlequin's mistress." Seed catalogues in Emily's time listed a few kinds of columbine in addition to the native variety. If you go to the nursery today, you'll find many new hybrids to choose from, including the big, showy "McKana's Giant" and the frilly "Nora Barlow." Lately, growers have introduced Japanese dwarf hybrids like "Nana" and "Blue Butterflies." At six inches tall, these miniatures are perfect for the front of your shady border.

Emily may have known the name "granny's bonnet," since this poem seems to be describing a wild columbine in bloom:

ᐁ

Glowing is her Bonnet -
Glowing is her Cheek -
Glowing is her Kirtle -
Yet she cannot speak.

Better as the Daisy
From the summer hill
Vanish unrecorded
Save by tearful rill -

Save by loving sunrise
Looking for her face.
Save by feet unnumbered
Pausing at the place.

(106B)

CROWN IMPERIAL *(Fritillaria imperialis)* Emily once wrote to her closest friend, Susan Gilbert, saying, "I have to go out in the garden now, and whip a Crown-Imperial for presuming to hold its head up, until you have come home."[34] This was quite the comparison, as the crown imperial dominates the late-spring sunny border with a stem as tall as a yard-stick, topped with a crown of green leaves and a coronet of large yellow or orange flowers.

Crown imperials grow from large bulbs that have a peculiar odor, a bit like skunk. The bulbs contain an alkaloid that gives some people a rash, so wear gloves when you plant them. Give them good drainage, moisture in the spring, and dryness in the summer. Once planted, don't disturb the bulbs as long as they keep up their annual bloom, as they are temperamental sorts. Was Emily implying that Susan was temperamental too? Who knows, but Susan would later marry Emily's brother, Austin.

DAFFODIL *(Narcissus spp.)* Being a lunatic on bulbs pays off. In spring, the long flower beds in Emily's garden also sported blooms of bulbs, like daffodils, that had been planted in autumn. In one poem, Emily tallies her spring garden like some Dickensian miser.

c2—

Then I have "shares" in Primrose "Banks" -
Daffodil Dowries - spicy "stocks" -
Dominions - broad as Dew -
Bags of Doubloons - adventurous Bees
Brought me - from firmamental seas -
And Purple - from Peru -

(266)

Like a growing dowry, some daffodil varieties come back each year with bigger numbers. If you're looking for that in your garden, read the catalogue descriptions for daffodils that say "perennializer" or "naturalizer." Emily must have grown those varieties to get the "seas of daffodils" that she describes in another poem.

Daffodils are all members of the genus *Narcissus*, named for a Greek swain who looked into a pool and fell in love with his own reflection before falling in. The gods took pity on him and turned him into a yellow flower, nodding over the water. The common names are a bit

---

⊰ **TIP** ⊱

Daffodils are undemanding. They don't like wet feet, but if the drainage is good, they'll happily bloom for years in sun or shade, rich soil or poor. If you are a neat gardener, daffodils look better with the spent blooms cut off. When the bloom is over, leave the strappy foliage to absorb energy for the bulb. The leaves will disappear by July. If you think the leaves look too forlorn, plant daffodils with something tall to cover them. In Emily's poem and garden, she used "spicy 'stocks,'" a tall annual, to cover the bare spots.

confusing. There are many different varieties, but "daffodil" and "narcissus" are synonyms that apply to all of them. "Jonquil" is another name commonly used, but is actually the term for a specific kind of daffodil.

PRIMROSE (*Primula spp.*) "Primrose banks" yield early interest in Emily's garden. Umbels of color bloom on short spikes. Emily could have chosen from whole palettes of primroses: cowslips and oxlips and varieties hailing from the highlands of Scotland and the mountains of Japan. Primroses are a hardy bunch. There is a chapter of the American Primrose Society in Alaska, as well as one in New England. While most primroses are oblivious to the cold, they dislike the heat. Give them some shade and water—they are particularly thirsty in the summer.

Many of the plants in Emily's garden were ground covers. This category of plant, beloved of gardeners, grows along the ground—choking out weeds along the way. Their flowers are a bonus.

Shares from Emily's primrose banks

LILY OF THE VALLEY (*Convallaria majalis*) Emily's niece Mattie describes carpets of lily of the valley that spread every year in Emily's garden. Emily also called it Vale Lily in one May letter, saying, "I said I should send some flowers this week. I had rather not until next week - My Vale Lily asked me to wait for her." [35]

Lily of the valley is a tough, hardy plant. It blooms with nodding white bells in May and grows even in full shade. Grow it for the fragrance; it may remind you of your grandmother's dusting powder. Just a small spray will scent a room. Mattie said that in the Dickinson gar-

---
⇥ **TIP** ⇤

Lily of the valley is an easy plant to share—just dig out a clump in the spring or fall. Make sure you get some roots and at least one "pip," or growing tip, on each division. If you're lucky, you'll find someone with the pink-flowering variety to make a trade. The only downside to a lily of the valley ground cover is that it takes a winter vacation, dying to the ground when it gets cold.

---

den they gathered it to decorate the family graves. But they must have brought some into the house, too.

MYRTLE (*Vinca minor*) Another ground cover plant, a favorite of Emily's mother, is myrtle. According to Mattie, her grandmother let it meander wherever it wanted. Its shiny oval leaves grow along runners (long stems that send out roots), spreading happily in sun or shade. Some people call it periwinkle because, as a bonus, it blooms with periwinkle blue flowers in April.

FORGET-ME-NOTS (*Myostotis sylvatica*) Blue forget-me-nots with yellow eyes bloomed in Emily's garden. They are biennial, growing one season, blooming and enthusiastically self-sowing the next. After the flowers mature, the stems elongate and you'll see small seeds forming where the flowers were. Even though the plants start to look a little messy, don't be too neat. You have to let the seeds ripen and fall to the ground. If you clean them up, you'll be taking away the seed. Forget-me-nots are pass-along plants. If you get it started in your garden, you'll soon have plenty of seedlings to give away. Emily once enclosed some of its flowers in a letter saying, "I send you a little Antidote to the love of others - Whenever you feel yourselves enticed, cling to its Admonition." [36]

Lilac (*Syringa vulgaris*) The lilacs in Emily's garden were laden with perfumed panicles of bloom in May. They scent the air, a delicious smell as enticing as cookies baking. It's impossible for people not to stick their noses in them. Lilacs are long-lived, and their purple flowers reminded Emily of the sunset and of her botanical glossary.

The Lilac is an ancient Shrub
But ancienter than that
The Firmamental Lilac
Opon the Hill tonight -
The Sun subsiding on his Course
Bequeaths this final plant
To Contemplation - not to Touch -
The Flower of Occident.

Of one Corolla is the West -
The Calyx is the Earth -
The Capsule's burnished Seeds the Stars -
The Scientist of Faith
His research has but just begun -
Above his Synthesis
The Flora unimpeachable
To Time's Analysis -
"Eye hath not seen" may possibly
Be current with the Blind
But let not Revelation
By Theses be detained -

(1261)

Emily poetically notes the "Capsule's burnished seeds." After lilac flowers fade, the remaining inflorescence develops into the seed pods, eventually turning brown. At this point, cut off the seed pods, signaling the plant to put its energy into leaf production. June is also the right time

---

⇒❙ TIP ❘⇐

Lilacs are undemanding plants. They will grow in sunny spots in prac-
tically any soil and, once established, don't ask for any extra water or
fertilizer, though they will reward you if you give them a dusting of
lime near their roots in spring. Unfortunately a fungus called powdery
mildew (*Microsphaera alni*) coats the leaves of many varieties of lilac
with white powder in late summer. It's a bit unsightly, but doesn't
harm the plant in any way. If you're choosing lilacs now, seek out vari-
eties that aren't susceptible. The color and scent of the May flowers
outweigh their problems in my book, and, I think, in Emily's—for
although she once called lilacs "delusive," they did remind her "Of
Idleness and Spring." [37]

---

to prune lilacs. Pruning them in winter will cut off the flower buds
because lilacs bloom on old, or last year's, wood. If you have a large,
overgrown bush, cut two or three large old branches right to the
ground and shorten the rest of the branches to about four feet. Then
you'll be able to see, smell and reach the lilacs as they bloom.

Sometimes spring seems impossibly busy. Emily lavished attention on
the garden, kneeling on a red army blanket when the ground was damp.
She often paused and picked a flower to savor.

A Late Spring Garden Primer

Pressed flowers are wonderful additions to your garden notebook or
photo album. Consider starting your own herbarium.

How to Create a Herbarium

If bees pirated nectar, then Emily pirated flowers to make her herbarium. To create a herbarium like Emily's, you start by collecting and pressing flowers.

THE WARNING LABEL   Emily had never heard the term "endangered species," but today collecting wildflowers is a real concern. Even then, though, Emily noticed that "There are not many wild flowers near, for

---

⊰ **THE BEES** ⊱ ---

Lilacs attract bees. In one letter, Emily writes, "I must just show you a Bee, that is eating a Lilac at the Window. There - there - he is gone! How glad his family will be to see him!" [38] The bee eating at Emily's lilac was a worker bee: actually a she, not a he, as all worker bees are female. She was gathering nectar for her family—the bee colony, back at the hive. Flowers produce nectar, a sweet liquid, as a come-hither for pollinators. As Emily's bee was collecting nectar, the key ingredient in honey, tiny particles of pollen were sticking to her body and lodging in "pollen baskets," special hairs on her back legs. The bee spread pollen from one flower to another accidentally as she moved from one to the next. And she took back pollen, another apian food, to the hive.

Emily's bee was one of many leaving the hive in spring. After the temperature is above freezing, bees begin flying in search of nectar and pollen to replenish supplies consumed over the winter.

She was fond of the bee as an ever-ready source of onomatopoeia, the use of a word that sounds like its meaning. Just as "moo" sounds like a cow, Emily called bees "Buccaneers of Buzz." [39] They pirated nectar from her spring garden.

---

the girls have driven them to a distance, and we are obliged to walk quite a distance to find them, but they repay us by their sweet smiles and fragrance." [40]

The responsible way to collect specimens for your herbarium is to grow them in your garden. Most "wildflowers" are available from reputable nurseries that propagate them according to guidelines established by the Nature Conservancy.

Many wildflowers growing in woods and meadows are disappearing. Their habitats are turning into strip malls and housing developments. But some flowers are common and can be collected guilt-free, like Queen Anne's lace—beautiful, but actually a native of Europe that escaped from early gardens. So if you want to collect flowers on botanizing excursions like Emily's, go armed with information. The native plant societies and wildflower nonprofit organizations are great sources of information, set up by state or region for the protection, appreciation, and study of native flora. If you're not sure about a flower that you find, it's best to follow the adage "take only pictures—leave only footprints."

THE PREPARATION The materials needed to make a herbarium are simple:

First, you'll need a flower press. In a pinch, you can use a phone book. But if you want to be official and have more reliable results, get a flower press. Many gardening supply catalogues sell them—there are even ones that work in the microwave if you'd like instant gratification.

To make a traditional flower press, go to the hardware store (or your garage) and get two pieces of plywood cut to the same size, either rectangular or square. Common sizes for presses are five inches by five inches, nine inches by nine inches, and eleven inches by seventeen inches. The size of the plants you want to collect determines the size of the press.

To apply the pressure that will flatten the plants, you can either use bungee cords or, more conventionally, drill the corners. Stack the two pieces together and drill a hole one-half inch from each corner.

On page twelve of her herbarium, Emily arranged three wildflowers that bloom across the year: fall-blooming wild sarsaparilla (*Aralia nudicaulis*), the spring ephemeral liverleaf (*Hepatica triloba*), and mullein (*Verbascum thapsus*), which blooms in summer.

Slide a long bolt through both pieces of wood in each of the four holes. Slide washers on top of the wood and twist a wing nut on the end of each bolt.

Cut sheets of blotting paper and corrugated cardboard slightly smaller than the press. The blotting paper will absorb the moisture from the flower, and the cardboard will separate the layers as they dry. For blotting paper, you can cut up sheets of newspaper, but it's best to use something unprinted right next to the plant to avoid transferring ink. White paper towels work beautifully.

Gather up your collecting kit. You'll need plastic zipper bags, scissors, and a permanent marker to take with you on your expedition.

THE SELECTION Pressing flowers is a process of preserving a living object and changing it from three dimensions into two.

Selecting which flowers to press is something of an art. Small, skinny flowers are the easiest. Big, fleshy ones, like daffodils, resist drying evenly. Single flowers, with one row of petals, look more natural than fluffy doubles, which come out looking squashed rather than pressed. Spring flowers from Emily's garden that are easy to press include violets and pansies.

To have the freshest materials to work with, cut the flowers or leaves in the morning, after the dew is dried. Put each specimen in a plastic bag. If you know the name of the plant, label the plastic bag with a permanent marker. Press the flowers as soon as you get them home, or bring your press with you. Once they've wilted, they're difficult to work with, and the likelihood you'll have a good product at the end is slim.

I held a Jewel in my fingers -
And went to sleep -
The day was warm, and winds were prosy -
I said "'Twill keep" -

I woke - and chid my honest fingers,
The Gem was gone -
And now, an Amethyst remembrance
Is all I own -

(261)

Place each flower or leaf on blotting paper. Flatten with your fingers and put another sheet of paper on top. Sandwich the paper, in turn, with two pieces of cardboard. Slide the stack in between the sheets of your press. Tighten the wing nuts to exert pressure.

Check the progress of your press once a week. It generally takes from two weeks to a month to press the flowers completely. Make sure the flowers are completely dried before you take them out of the press. You may find that their colors have changed somewhat during the drying process—white fades to ivory, red to a deep burgundy. It's part of the charm.

THE LAYOUT　Now you are ready to arrange your specimens. You can place one per page or make an arrangement on a page as Emily did. Mount the specimens with Post-it strips or paper tape over bits of stem. Don't glue down the whole flower or plant—glue gets too brittle.

Label each herbarium specimen. This is an opportunity to practice your penmanship. The standard herbarium label includes the plant family, the botanical name, the common name, the location, and the date. But unless you're collecting as a scientific pursuit, be creative! The Victorians often labeled a pressed plant with something poetic: a phrase like "Be true" or a word like "Remembrance."

If you don't want to mount your flowers, store them flat in envelopes or books. They can join paper in collages or be covered with ink on a stamp pad (vein side down) and printed. Pressed petals, as Emily knew, make lovely enclosures for cards or letters. They are also perfect in handmade paper.

I pay - in Satin Cash -
You did not state - your price -
A Petal, for a Paragraph
Is near as I can guess -

(526)

Once you have tried pressing flowers, you can be expansive about
what to press. Ferns, leaves, and seaweed are excellent candidates.

EARLY SUMMER

A Gardener's Homecoming

On a mellow, warm evening in June, the French doors are flung open, their panes reflecting the trees and the lawn in the uneven ripples of Victorian glass. The faint sound of a piano drifts over from a neighbor's parlor. It is undeniably summer.

After supper, the sun is still high enough to light the interior of the double parlor, cutting an angled swath on the wooden floorboards. Dust motes hang in the air even though spring cleaning is just finished. The windows shine; the carpets have been beaten and rolled up for the summer. Blankets are airing on the clothesline behind the kitchen. Summarizing her attitude toward housework, Emily said succinctly, "I prefer pestilence." [1] She always preferred gardening.

Summer was Emily's favorite season. She mentions it more than any other—there are 145 references to summer in her poems. Its closest competitor, winter, shows a mere thirty-nine. She is a poet of seasonal extremes.

It will be Summer - eventually.
Ladies - with parasols -
Sauntering Gentlemen - with Canes -
And little Girls - with Dolls -

Will tint the pallid landscape -
As 'twere a bright Boquet -
Tho' drifted deep, in Parian -
The Village lies - today -

The Lilacs - bending many a year -
Will sway with purple load -
The Bees - will not despise the tune -
Their Forefathers - have hummed -

The Wild Rose - redden in the Bog -
The Aster - on the Hill
Her everlasting fashion - set -
And Covenant Gentians - frill -

Till Summer folds her miracle -
As Women - do - their Gown -
Or Priests - adjust the Symbols -
When Sacrament - is done -

(374B)

Travels of a Gardener

As much as a gardener loves a patch of ground, travel is tempting. In her teens and early twenties, Emily traveled away from her village many times.

In Boston, she visited her Aunt Lavinia and Uncle Loring Nor-
cross, playing the tourist at the Chinese Museum, the Statehouse, and
Bunker Hill. As a gardener and a romantic, she was most interested in
Mount Auburn Cemetery. To our present-day sensibilities, it seems
odd to add a graveyard to a sightseeing itinerary, but in Emily's day it
was thought of as another sort of park. She and her relatives would
have walked in through the granite Egyptian gate on Mount Auburn
Street.

Emily meandered around curving roads, by ponds reflecting their
appropriately weeping willows, and up Mount Auburn for the wide
view of the Charles River and Boston beyond. The land was sculpted
around ancient black oaks and planted with ornamental trees like pur-
ple European beeches; the plots themselves were marked with elegant
sculpture or iron fences. Yet the graves blended with the picturesque
landscape, as if on returning to dust, individual identities merged back
into Nature. Emily bequeathed her impressions to us.

"Have you ever been to Mount Auburn?" she wrote. "If not you can
form but slight conception - of the 'City of the dead.' It seems as if
Nature had formed the spot with a distinct idea in view of its being a
resting place for her children, where wearied & disappointed they
might stretch themselves beneath the spreading cypress & close their
eyes 'calmly as to a nights repose or flowers at set of sun.'" [2]

Aunt Lavinia also took her niece to the Saturday display of fruits,
flowers, and vegetables at the rooms of the Massachusetts Horticultural
Society.

The spectacular floral exhibits were a sort of Victorian Tourna-
ment of Roses parade. Emily the gardener was inspired by full-scale ver-
sions of a Grecian floral temple, a Swiss cottage decorated with moss
and flowers, a pagoda—complete with a Chinese tea merchant and fin-
ished with fuchsias—and a Gothic monument fourteen feet tall. There
were huge arrangements displayed in vases and hung on walls. One that
Emily saw was "a beautiful flat fancy design of large dimensions, pre-
senting a surface wrought with asters, amaranths, and other flowers,
with the words 'Horticultural Exhibition, 1846' inscribed in a border

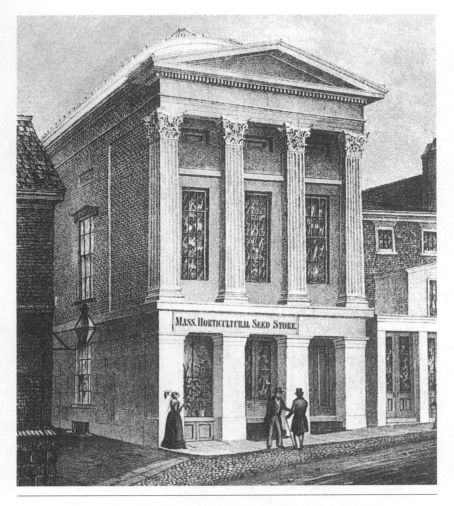

Horticultural Hall, where Emily saw the exhibition in 1846

around it, wrought with immortal flowers." [3] So many ideas to take home to Amherst.

Like any good gardener, Emily worried about what was happening in her own garden while she was away. Was it adequately watered? What blooms was she missing out on? "Do you have any flowers in Norwich?" she asked Abiah Root. "My garden looked finely when I left home. It is in Viny's [sic] care during my absence." [4] Emily solved the gardener's dilemma by delegating maintenance to her baby sister.

Off to College

Mount Holyoke Female Seminary, later renamed Mount Holyoke College, was the setting for Emily's longest time away from home. It was September 1847; she was almost seventeen. Trunk packed and loaded into the family carriage, they pulled out of Amherst. The horses' hooves churned a wake of dust all the way to South Hadley. They passed a familiar landscape, farms and mills, and rattled through the covered bridge that crossed the Fort River. As they pulled up to the large white building that housed the Seminary, it must have seemed far away from home and garden, though it was actually only ten miles.

She roomed with her cousin, Emily Norcross, in the upstairs dormitory. Their room, simply furnished and lit with whale-oil lamps, was too cold for houseplants, even with the Franklin stove. "How do the plants look now & are they flourishing as before I went away?" she asked Austin in November. "I wish much to see them. Some of the girls here, have plants, but it is a cold place & I am very glad that I did not bring any, as I thought of doing." [5]

She left Mount Holyoke after a year, telling a friend that Father had decided not to send her back. If that seems peculiar, some hint of future reclusiveness, keep in mind that women seldom attended college in those days, and even fewer finished.

Just a few years later, in 1853, Mr. Dickinson went to Washington as a newly elected United States congressman, giving Emily the opportunity for her next major excursion, this time with Vinnie. During three weeks in the city, they were most impressed with Mount Vernon and the tomb of George Washington. It must have been unusually warm that year. "Sweet and soft as summer . . . maple trees in bloom and grass green in the sunny places," Emily wrote to her friends. [6]

At one point during the trip, Austin teased his sisters, "He says we forget 'the Horse, the Cats, and the geraniums,'" Emily wrote to a friend. "(He) . . . proposes to sell the farm and move west with mother - to make bouquets of my plants, and send them to his friends." But Emily counters, "as for my sweet flowers, I shall know each leaf and every bud that bursts, while I am from home." [7]

Home Is Where the Garden Is

By 1855, Emily was able to celebrate summer in her garden at the origi-
nal Homestead on Main Street. When it had come back on the market
that past winter, Edward, now established in his law practice as well as
in politics, grabbed the chance. He was buying back the house his father
lost, reasserting his birthright via a real estate transaction. Samuel
Fowler Dickinson's ghost was assuaged.

Emily's father acquired the brick house, outbuildings, ample
property around the house, and the eleven-plus acre meadow across the
street. He sank at least as much money into renovations, adding Ital-
ianate features: a cupola, French doors, the piazza, architraves over the
windows in the paired parlors, marble mantels for the fireplaces. It took
the better part of a year for the carpenters and masons to finish their
work.

So Emily and her family uprooted themselves from the North
Pleasant Street house and garden and moved back to the Homestead.
She mused, "I supposed we were going to make a 'transit,' as heavenly
bodies did - but we came budget by budget, as our fellows do, till we
fulfilled the pantomime contained in the word 'moved.' It is a kind of
gone-to-Kansas feeling, and if I sat in a long wagon, with my family tied
behind, I should suppose without doubt I was a party of emigrants!"[8]
Coming through the front door, a silver doorplate welcomed them.

She took some time to get used to living there again. "They say
that 'home is where the heart is,'" she wrote. "I think it is where the *house*
is, and the adjacent buildings."[9] But Emily soon rediscovered her
favorite nooks. There is a hallway that links the kitchen with the formal
front rooms. Mattie remembers her calling it "the Northwest passage,"
an elusive but profitable channel. It was one of her favorite retreats,
with five exits that included a back stairway and a door to the garden.
A friend of the family remembered, "She received me in a little back
hall that connected with the kitchen. It was dimly lighted. She asked if
I would have a glass of wine or a rose. I told her I would take the rose,
and she went to the garden and brought one in to me. She seemed very

unusual, and her voice, her looks, and her whole personality made an impression on me that is still very vivid after all these years." [10]

Home may be where the house is, but it is definitely where the *garden* is, and Emily was soon collecting quantities of flowers from the Homestead's gardens. In these years, Emily enjoyed calling in Amherst, leaving her calling card and often a bouquet. Since families had reserved seats on Sundays at the First Parish Meeting House (the Congregational Church), sometimes she would creep in early and deposit bouquets for friends in their families' pews.

We would call Emily's bouquets "nosegays" or "tussie-mussies." She made them of a great variety of flowers, pressed close together in concentric circles, and taped or tied to hold them in place. Cutting the flowers in the evening, she would let the stems sit in water overnight, drinking to their maximum. She got creative. "On one occasion a friend received a more formal and more elaborate bouquet than usual, with a line of admonition in regard to one flower. Upon examination, and the

A nosegay like the ones Emily made

removal of the flower, a tiny note was found wound around the stem, carefully concealed from view." [11]

The Pen and the Trowel

Emily was writing more than little notes to hide in bouquets. This was the period when she first wrote a significant number of poems. She sat at one of two small square cherry writing desks, one in her father's study looking out onto the garden, and the other in her bedroom. From the front windows of her bedroom she gazed over the Dickinson meadow and beyond to the Pelham Hills and the Holyoke Range.

Dipping her pen in a dark ink well, she wrote words. A word became a construct, part memory, part imagination. Embedded in a poem, with meter and rhyme, the words became like the petals of a rose, each different, but creating a cadence and a symmetry.

She was both writer and reader, and among her readings were selections about gardens, flowers, and nature. During Emily's life, garden writing flourished as technology fueled printing, and gardening first became America's pastime. Emily read Thoreau and Emerson, those bards of eastern Massachusetts, and shared their propensity for transcending humdrum life by focusing on nature. She read gardening-related articles in more general magazines, like the *Atlantic Monthly*, to which the Dickinsons subscribed. A gardener who reads never gardens alone.

In Harvard's Houghton Library, you can still see a book that her father gave her when she was twenty-eight, called *Wildflowers Drawn and Colored from Nature.* He inscribed it "To my daughter Emily from her father Edw. Dickinson January 1, 1859." It is a book by a woman, Mrs. C. M. Badger, a large folio with sentimental poems and illustrations of flowers. With its embossed cover and subject matter, it must have made a lovely companion to the herbarium. And I think, somehow, that her father must have wanted to encourage her with this example of a woman writer and artist.

As well as writing and reading, after moving back to the house on Main Street, Emily settled back into making her garden.

Early Summer in Emily Dickinson's Garden

↩

"Endless summer days -"

(207B)

Step through the French doors of the Homestead onto the piazza and find yourself among the potted plants. The oleanders in their green tubs have been lugged out from the conservatory, their thin shiny leaves building energy for an August bloom. They are joined by the daphne, which bloomed all winter under glass and is enthusiastically setting new bud.

Summer reaches out, high tide for the garden. Walking around the back of the house, you can see Emily's inspiration for yourself.

↩

My Garden - like the Beach -
Denotes there be - a Sea -
That's Summer -
Such as These - the Pearls
She fetches - such as Me

(469)

With the trees leafed out, they shade Emily, as well as her house and yard. The leaves riffle in the breeze, like water moving over rocks in a slow current. Having lost their spring florescence, they darken with a concentration of chlorophyll. The oaks are subtly flowering, shedding dusty pollen on the flagstones of the garden path.

The honeysuckle twines up a trellis just outside the study, its scent taking over where the lilacs left off. Two honeysuckle arbors arch over the garden path. New plants need to be coaxed onto their supports, a snake charmer's art. Emily sometimes took on the job: "I went out before tea tonight, and trained the Honeysuckle - it grows very fast and finely." [12] And other times her sister did it. "Vinnie trains the Honeysuckle - and the Robins steal the string for Nests - quite, quite as they used to." [13]

A hummingbird is summoned by the nectar in its tubular flowers. You might hear the whir of wings before you see the bird. It hovers above a target bloom and sticks a long cake-tester tongue in to sample the sweetness.

It is a lovely evening for a walk in the garden. The light is delicious.

Honeysuckle

∽

Morning - is the place for Dew -
Corn - is made at Noon -
After dinner light - for flowers -
Dukes - for setting sun!

(223)

Hedges of peonies nod their languorous heads in the upper garden. Ants march steadily on the unopened buds, like suitors courting a debutante. If there has been a heavy rain, there is havoc in the peony hedge. Water weights the blooms, pulling down stems.

The sword leaves of the iris seem to be moving faster than the breeze. One of Vinnie's cats is stalking a small rodent among the rhizomes.

⤔ CATS IN THE GARDEN ⇤

Lavinia loved her cats and christened them with silly names like Drummydoodles, pedestrian names like Tabby, and names that prefigured *Entertainment Today,* such as Buffy and Tootsie. It's hard to imagine gardening with all of them around.

There are some upsides. Cats hunt rodents, so the population of voles, chipmunks, and other burrowing beasts will go down in inverse proportion to the felines in the neighborhood.

The most contentious issues between gardeners and cats seem to come down to two opposite ends of the kitty digestive tract. First, cats will eat, roll in, and otherwise destroy plants of their liking such as (not surprisingly) catmint and catnip. And if you, like Emily, are a lover of birds, you will not appreciate the feline fondness for avian murder. At the other end of their digestive tract, tilled garden soil becomes the great outdoor litter box.

If you want to banish the beasts, avoid planting cat magnets. You can try using water pistols, animal repellent sprays, usually garlic and hot pepper–based, or mechanical solutions like prickly plants or eggshells.

Vinnie's solution was an interesting one. Having your own outdoor cat (or cats) will sometimes do the trick. They are less likely to sully their own turf and will patrol their territory to keep their fellows at bay.

To Vinnie's cats, the garden was a hunting ground.

The bloom stalks of the iris stand up stiffly, buds unfurling. Emily noted their piquant odor.

⌒

Bright Flowers slit a Calyx
And soared opon a stem
Like Hindered Flags - Sweet hoisted -
With Spices - in the Hem -

(523)

Down the flagstone path, the fruit trees are beginning to set. Cherries, apples, plums, and pears, still in miniature, have usurped the place of the spring blooms. The three cherry trees closest to the house will be the first to ripen. Delicious just picked, once pitted the cherries will yield pies for the table. The fruit attracts the birds, taking bids on the sugary drupes.

In addition to fruit trees, the Dickinson garden also had a strawberry bed. The classic varieties Emily cultivated bore heavily for a few weeks in June, sometimes a quart per plant. It was time for pies, cakes, and preserves, the smell of cooking strawberries drifting out of the kitchen door and into the garden, inducing salivation.

⌒

Over the fence -
Strawberries - grow -
Over the fence -
I could climb - if I tried, I know -
Berries are nice!

But - if I stained my Apron -
God would certainly scold!
Oh, dear, - I guess if He were a Boy -
He'd - climb - if he could!

(271)

"Berries are nice!"

⚜ STRAWBERRY FIELDS ⚜

Picking strawberries may be an event, but growing them is a process. Pick a sunny location with good drainage. Set your plants eighteen inches apart, and mulch to keep the weeds down. Pinch off the blossoms the first year to allow the plants to build strength for bearing fruit the second. Fertilize every year at blossom time with a top dressing of well-rotted (or bagged) manure. Keep the bed well weeded. Each "mother" plant will send out shoots like spider plants. Cut these off and set them out in a separate bed.

Mulch all of the plants in the winter with straw or salt hay. Remove the mulch the next spring, and get ready for your June harvest. You may want to put netting or cheesecloth over the plants when they blossom to avoid having the birds and chipmunks abscond with your berries. Don't pick the fruit until it is ripe—the fruit won't continue to ripen once it is severed from the plant. Right after harvest, cut down all of the foliage to one and a half inches; use a hedge shears or lawn mower, depending on the size of your beds. Replace half of the mother plants with offspring from the nursery bed. And enjoy the taste of summer.

Strawberry runners

In the flower garden, climbing roses luxuriate on the arbors and the latticework summer house, and old-fashioned shrub roses stretch out into the path, covered with blossoms. Perennials are at peak, and annuals fill in, steady and undemanding. Let's take a stroll with Emily to see what's in bloom.

A Little Catalogue of Early Summer Flowers

Roses are the dominant note in the flower garden this season.

The Roses

If summer was her favorite season, roses were Emily's favorite flower. She mentions them in letters, for example, a tea rose bush that Vinnie gave to her namesake, Aunt Lavinia. And always looking for a clever turn of phrase, she wrote to one correspondent, "Vinnie picked the *Sub rosas* in your note and handed them to me."[14] She often appropriated roses for her poems, like the subject of this verse:

Pigmy seraphs - gone astray -
Velvet people from Vevay -
Belles from some lost summer day -
Bees exclusive Coterie -

Paris could not lay the fold
Belted down with emerald -
Venice could not show a cheek
Of a tint so lustrous meek -
Never such an ambuscade
As of briar and leaf displayed
For my little damask maid -

I had rather wear her grace
Than an Earl's distinguished face -
I had rather dwell like her
Than be "Duke of Exeter" -
Royalty enough for me
To subdue the Bumblebee.

(96B)

This poem is Emily's Grand Tour, complete with imagined meetings, hospitable hosts, and capitals and resorts on the Continent. Paris, Venice, even English royalty didn't overshadow a stroll among her roses.

To last through cold New England winters, roses in Emily's garden needed to be hardy, but there were many varieties that fit the bill. Today, our rose sensibilities have narrowed to a florist's definition—roses are long-stemmed, usually red and sold by the dozen, with fat blooms and little scent. But the genus *Rosa* has a big family tree. The species that grew in Emily's garden are still available today from specialty growers (see the Resources).

DAMASK ROSE (*Rosa damascena*) Emily's "damask maid" is one of a class called damask roses. Their modest, three-inch roses open in clusters of flattened rosettes. The shoots are thorny, "an ambuscade" especially for the gardener trying to clip some blooms. They are an ancient rose, cultivated for centuries in the Middle East and by Romans in the Empire, and resurrected by the French. The flowers subdue the bees with their fragrance.

GREVILLE ROSE (*Rosa multiflora grevillei*) Emily's mother brought the Greville rose with her to Amherst as a new bride in 1828. If you read the Household Cyclopedia of General Information, published in 1881, you'll find a reference to the Greville rose. It was bred in 1816 and was a popular climber from then on. The large double flowers open in lavish trusses, and their color may stop visitors in their tracks. In the same

cluster individual blooms range from pale pink to magenta. Aficiona-
dos thought that there were seven shades of pink and dubbed the plant
the "Seven Sisters" rose.

HEDGEHOG ROSE (*Rosa rugosa rubra*) A hedgehog is a spiny crea-
ture—we'd probably call it a porcupine. It's a good metaphor for the
rugosa rose, which is equally prickly. Although it is native to northern
China, the Korean peninsula, and the archipelago of Japan, it has natu-
ralized across the New England dunes, suggesting its other moniker, the
salt spray rose. Its botanical name, *rugosa*, describes the wrinkled,
rugose look of its glossy green leaves.

⤙ TIP ⤚

For those of you who don't have the time or inclination to fuss with a
rose, the rugosa is for you. It has no special taste for fertilizer regi-
mens or extra watering. It is tough. It's even amenable to some shade.
The only thing you need to give it is good drainage; so if you have
heavy clay soil, mix in some peat moss, sand, or compost before you
plant it. It will reward you with fragrant single flowers: white, pink,
yellow, or purple, depending on the cultivar. And in the fall, the rose
hips that remain after the petals fall will turn bright red.

BLUSH ROSE (*Rosa* "Old Blush") The blush is a China rose, first intro-
duced in the nursery trade in the 1740s, well after Emily's ancestors had
settled around Amherst. Like those Dickinson forebears, the China rose
passed on its traits to countless offspring and hybrids. "Old Blush" is a
vigorous shrub, its lilac blooms standing in soft clusters that darken to
mauve in the sun. Emily would have known that they didn't make good

cut flowers. The petals fall quickly, so she would have left on the hips
and been rewarded with the glow of their orange orbs in the fall.

Cinnamon Rose (*Rosa cinnamomea* or *Rosa majalis*) Her niece, Mattie, tells us that Emily grew "a variety of single rose they called the Cinnamon rose—renamed by our generation Love-for-a-day roses because
they flare and fall between sunrise and sunset." [15] The cinnamon rose,
native to southern Europe, was first offered for sale circa 1600. Its
extract was taken as a tonic in ancient times. In Emily's garden it is an
upright rose bush with grey-green leaves and single soft pink flowers
that open in early June.

Calico Rose (*Rosa gallica* "Versicolor") It does look like calico or
chintz, but this rose is actually named for the French. But "gallica," "calico"—you can see where the common name came from. A number of
cultivars of the *gallica* have variegated petals, their "fabric" striped with
pink, white, and magenta.

Sweetbrier Rose (*Rosa eglanteria*) In Shakespeare's *A Midsummer
Night's Dream*, Titiana is lulled to sleep under a canopy of eglantine, or
sweetbrier rose. When Emily mentions her mother's sweetbrier, she is
referring to a huge shrub rose with single pink flowers. If she rubbed
the leaves of the sweetbrier, they exuded a fragrance like sliced apples.
In the fall, like so many species roses, it put on a show of ruby hips.

The "Perennials"

Emily often compared perennial plants with resurrection and eternity.
Beyond the metaphor, the flowers that came back every year in her summer garden were actually a combination of plants: perennials, biennials, and bulbs.

Pinks (*Dianthus caryophyllus*) In a letter Emily queried jokingly,
"How is your garden - Mary? Are the Pinks true - and the Sweet

Williams faithful?" [16] The edges of pinks
are zigzag, like a seam that has been
trimmed with pinking shears. Their gray
strappy leaves grow in a mat. Their small
pink flowers are edible; they can be lovely
sprinkled on top of cheese or frozen into
ice cubes for tea. Sometimes Emily calls
them gillyflowers from the French word
for cloves, since they smell spicy. Her
forebears would have used them to flavor
wine and ale.

"Are the Pinks true?"

SWEET WILLIAMS (*Dianthus barbatus*) The sweet williams, another
cottage garden flower, open in shades of white, pink, and magenta. In
Emily's garden, the sweet williams sometimes were unfaithful, disap-
pearing after a year or two. But if she planted new seeds each summer,
they'd behave biennially, growing green one year and blooming the next.

ᐁ

When Diamonds are a Legend,
And Diadems - a Tale -
I Brooch and Earrings for Myself,
Do sow, and Raise for sale -

And tho' I'm scarce accounted,
My Art, a Summer Day - had Patrons -
Once - it was a Queen -
And once - a Butterfly -

(553)

POPPIES (*Papaver spp.*) Poppies have bible-thin petals; their wiry stems
bear heads that bob in the breeze. If they are happy in the garden, they

will often sow seeds from their ornamental seedheads and pop up in unexpected places. The red Oriental poppies look like miniature suns.

It was a quiet seeming Day -
There was no harm in earth or sky -
Till with the setting sun
There strayed an accidental Red
A strolling Hue, one would have said
To westward of the Town -

But when the Earth begun to jar
And Houses vanished with a roar
And Human Nature hid
We comprehended by the Awe
As those that Dissolution saw
The Poppy in the Cloud -

(1442)

DAISIES (*Chrysanthemum leucanthemum*) White daisies with their yellow eyes contrast with red poppies. Emily associated with them, using Daisy as a nickname for herself in letters. The daisies that Emily grew and that still populate the fields around Amherst are ox-eye daisies. While Emily adored them, not everyone agreed. One of her relatives once said, "Why do people rave over the beauty of daisies? They look to me like hard-boiled eggs cut in two." [17] Gardeners are notorious for strong opinions about particular flowers.

LILIES (*Lilium spp.*) As summer progresses, lilies start to bloom with fanfare. The bulbs throw up dense tufts of green each spring and their trumpet-shaped flowers open reliably year after year. Emily grew a selection of lily types; Mattie tells us of Japanese lilies, yellow lilies, tiger lilies, Madonna lilies, and one alluring, unnamed variety: "a white one with rose-powdered petals and brown velvet stamens, far more elaborate than the simple varieties of her mother's choice." [18] They are a spectacle in Emily's garden for weeks.

Emily did have a way with lilies. One spring when she was staying with her cousins Louisa ("Loo") and Frances ("Fanny") Norcross, she wrote to Vinnie, "The Pink Lily you gave Loo, has had five flowers since I came, and has more Buds. The Girls think it my influence." [19]

References to "Consider the lilies," a Biblical phrase (Luke 12:27; Matthew 6:28), appear a half-dozen times in her letters, often with gifts of the flowers. With a flair for exaggeration, she once confessed "the only Commandment I ever obeyed - 'Consider the Lilies.'" [20]

TIGER LILY (*Lilium tigrinum*) If tiger lilies have their spots, shouldn't they be leopard lilies? In spite of that, they are far from ferocious. Each orange petal is recurved like a gymnast doing a backbend on a parallel bar.

Clipper ships carried tiger lilies to America from European growers in the 1830s. The Chinese had grown them for centuries before that; they cooked and ate the bulbs. In the West, the flower was admired, not eaten.

FOXGLOVE (*Digitalis purpurea*) Like the lily, foxgloves are a vertical accent in Emily's early summer garden. From fuzzy leaves around the base of the plant, the magenta buds open along upright stems like pink obelisks. Flowers of fairy tales, they are called fox, or folk's, gloves for the fairies and elves. Each small bloom looks inviting to fingers; even the botanical name, *digitalis*, refers to fingers, our ten digits. Look inside the blooms and you'll see lovely spotting, a neon sign outside a bar for bees.

While it was unusual for Emily to have a poem published, one appeared in 1861 in the *Springfield Republican* with the title "The May Wine." It employs foxglove and bees; Emily's poetic response to Emerson's "The Poet": "The poet knows that he speaks adequately then only when he speaks somewhat wildly, or 'with the flower of the mind'; not

---

⊰‖ **TIP** ‖⊱

If you like your border to be tidy, then tiger lilies might not be the thing for you. They grow on four- to six-foot stems with strappy leaves, and bounce with gaudy charm over the rest of your flowers. But loosen up! They're charming. Plus their nectar is a favorite of swallowtail butterflies.

Tiger lilies are sun worshippers. But other than sunshine and good drainage, you can plant them and forget them. They'll do their thing every year.

If you have a friend with tiger lilies, ask if you can swipe some "bulbils," the little round black buttons that populate the leaf nodes right along the stem. If you put them on top of soil and water them, you'll be rewarded with new plants. Not hard to extrapolate that the tiger lily naturalized across the country, vying with our North American turk's cap lily for king of the meadow.

---

with the intellect used as organ, but with the intellect released from all service and suffered to take its direction from its celestial life; or as the ancients were wont to express themselves, not with the intellect alone but with the intellect inebriated by nectar." [21] Emily's antiphon was ecstatic:

I taste a liquor never brewed -
From Tankards scooped in Pearl -
Not all the Frankfort Berries
Yield such an Alcohol!

Inebriate of air - am I -
And Debauchee of Dew -
Reeling - thro' endless summer days -
From inns of molten Blue -

When "Landlords" turn the drunken Bee
Out of the Foxglove's door -
When Butterflies - renounce their "drams" -
I shall but drink the more!

Till Seraphs swing their snowy Hats -
And Saints - to windows run -
To see the little Tippler
Leaning against the - Sun

(207B)

The "Foxglove's door"

The Annuals

Annuals are the workhorses of Emily's summer borders. While the perennials return every year for a repeat performance, with rare exception they bloom for a few weeks and then turn into green blobs for the rest of the season. An annual, on the other hand, is determined to set seed this season, so it blooms its heart out until frost. A combination of annuals and perennials such as Emily and Vinnie had in their garden ensures that something is always in bloom.

SNAPDRAGON (*Antirrhinum majus*) The snapdragons take over from the foxgloves in late June and early July, rising with spires of pink, white, and magenta, even yellow. They seem more affectionate than their persnickety name suggests. If you squeeze the back of a bloom, it will open and close. When you plant snapdragons, be sure to give them a pinch. If you cut off the top half of every plant, they will reward you by branching out into bushy glory.

⇥| TIP |⇤

Foxgloves open their doors every June in the garden by sowing their seed and growing on into the autumn. There is something almost inexpressibly satisfying about self-sowers. They appeal to the little corner of Yankee thrift that inhabits the heart of every gardener by dropping free seed. In summer, you find free plants popping up that can be moved or given away.

For those of us who are horticultural control freaks, self-sowers also loosen up a garden. New gardens can be stiff, tightly planted in symmetrical groupings or rows. The volunteer seedlings materialize wherever they like the conditions, adding a repeating element to the garden and tying things together.

So don't be too neat. Wait until the seed pods that form behind the foxgloves' flowers are dry, then crush them between your fingers to release the tiny seeds around the garden. You'll see the fuzzy seedlings emerge when the weather cools in the fall, and when it warms up next spring.

SWEET ALYSSUM (*Lobularia maritima*) If summer is the sea, then alyssum is the foam on the waves. It is a tiny plant, only about three inches tall, with a haze of minute flowers—most often white, but also pink and purple. They smell sweet and add a lacy trimming along the front edge of a flower garden. If you have a flagstone path, sow sweet alyssum seeds in between the stones. They like to send their roots down next to the stones into the cool damp spaces. Alyssum will often self-sow if it's happy. Emily gathered seeds of sweet alyssum and mignonette from her fall garden to grow indoors over the winter.

MIGNONETTE (*Reseda odorata*) Mignonette is pronounced with the accent firmly on the "-ette," emphasizing as only the French can the

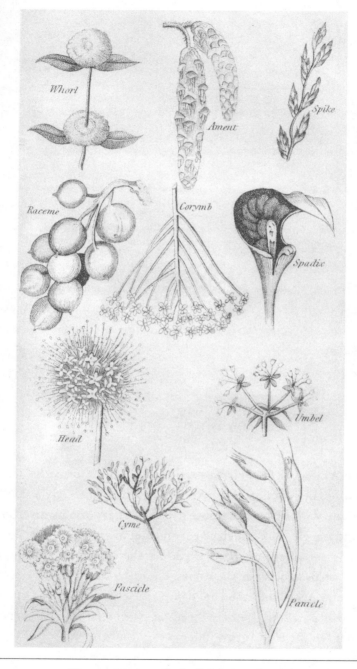

Flower structures in Emily's botany book

diminutive size of the flowers. The inflorescence is evasive, small, and inconspicuous to the eye. It is downright demure. But the flowers broadcast their fragrance like a Bloomingdale's perfume counter. Walking through her garden, the scent of mignonette would have wafted over to Emily, directing the eye to follow the nose. Brought inside to scent a bouquet, it was the Victorian equivalent of an aerosol air freshener. It's still grown commercially in France for the perfume industry. You won't find mignonette in anything but a specialty nursery, so if you want it in your garden, you'll need to grow it each year from seed.

STOCK (*Matthiola incana*) This flowery member of the mustard family is grown for its fragrant pastel flowers that look like clusters of miniature roses. It blooms in early summer on grey-green foliage. There are tall varieties for cutting, medium varieties for the border, and dwarf varieties for edging. Like Goldilocks, you can choose the one that is just right for your garden. To get a bushy plant, pinch the terminal bud. That will send the plant a message to branch out from the side of the stem, resulting in more shoots and more flowers.

Stocks

SWEET SULTAN (*Centaurea moschata*) If we only knew the potentate for which the flower is named. Sweet sultans are fragrant, hardy annuals that grow in the warm weather, blooming with flowers that look a bit like thistles. In Emily's time, sweet sultans were most often pink, but now you can also buy seeds of white and yellow varieties. Sow them "in place," in other words, right in the garden bed, because they pout if transplanted. They grow up as tall as a yardstick, so keep them toward the back of the border and use them for cutting. They keep flowering until frost if you deadhead regularly.

————————————⇥ **TEA TIME FOR PLANTS** ⇤————————————

Gardeners in Emily's day used manure tea to fertilize their annuals. To make this home brew, take an old pillowcase or a piece of burlap and put a quart of well-rotted cow manure inside. (If you don't happen to have a cow, you can buy a tidy bag at your local garden supply store.) Tie the top of the pillowcase and put it in a large bucket. Add two gallons of water. Let it steep overnight. It should be the color of strong coffee. Add two tablespoons of Epsom salts (high in magnesium) and two more gallons of water. Use your concoction within a week. Water your plants with manure tea, and see how they grow.

Plants Beyond the Garden Beds

Emily's summer wanderlust led her to the water and woods around Amherst, exploring and collecting.

ROCK POLYPODY FERN (*Polypodium virginianum*) By June, the ferns stand in clumps, their fiddleheads completely unfurled. Amherst's nineteenth-century naturalists, amateur and otherwise, dug them up and pressed them, bringing a bit of nature indoors. In one letter Emily wrote, "I bring you a Fern from my own Forest - where I play every Day." [22] The fern enclosed in the letter was a rock polypody, a small native that grows on moist rocks and in rock walls. If you turn the fern over, you see round sori, its spore-bearing polka dots, all over the underside. Ferns were part of the unfolding of the season.

～

An altered look about the hills -
A Tyrian light the village fills -
A wider sunrise in the morn -
A deeper twilight on the lawn -
A print of a vermillion foot -
A purple finger on the slope -
A flippant fly opon the pane -
A spider at his trade again -
An added strut in Chanticleer -
A flower expected everywhere -
An axe shrill singing in the woods -
Fern odors on untravelled roads -
All this and more I cannot tell -
A furtive look you know as well -
And Nicodemus' Mystery
Receives its annual reply!

(90)

MUSHROOMS (*Fungi*) It is mushroom season. It seems like they pop up overnight, a characteristic that Emily noticed. In her day, the mushroom was classified with the plant kingdom, rather than with fungi. Today's botany informs us that the mushroom is well-connected, with vast underground networks, like an extended family. Gazing at a mushroom is a prurient affair, given that it is the reproductive organ of a much larger plant.

～

The Mushroom is the Elf of Plants -
At Evening, it is not
At Morning, in a Truffled Hut
It stop opon a Spot

As if it tarried always
And yet its whole Career
Is shorter than a Snake's Delay -
And fleeter than a Tare -

'Tis Vegetation's Juggler -
The Germ of Alibi -
Doth like a Bubble antedate
And like a Bubble, hie -

I feel as if the Grass was pleased
To have it intermit -
This surreptitious Scion
Of Summer's circumspect.

Had Nature any supple Face
Or could she one contemn -
Had Nature an Apostate -
That Mushroom - it is Him!

(1350F)

THE POND LILY AND THE COW LILY (*Nymphaea odorata* and *Nuphar lutea*) In the wetlands the waterlilies are in full bloom. Waterlilies are ancient plants, primitives, never leaving the marshes where they evolved. Once, when her classmates dubbed Vinnie "the Pond Lily," Emily said, "Then I am the Cow Lily." [23] Like the two Dickinson sisters, both waterlilies are from the same family but are very different. The pond lily, like Vinnie, is showy, with large white flowers up to six inches across. Emily's cow lily is subdued, with small, waxy yellow flowers that grow in the shallows of ponds and lakes and in sluggish streams. The leaves look like underwater lettuce. Both have long roots that anchor the plants in the mud of ponds and stream shallows.

Will there really be a "morning"?
Is there such a thing as "Day"?
Could I see it from the mountains
If I were tall as they?

Has it feet like Water lilies?
Has it feathers like a Bird?
Is it brought from famous countries
Of which I have never heard?

Oh some Scholar! Oh some Sailor!
Oh some Wise Man from the skies!
Please to tell a little Pilgrim
Where the place called "morning" lies!

(148)

RED CLOVER (*Trifolium retense*) The Dickinson meadow is full of red clover, brought to America by the English colonists for their cattle. It is a preferred flower of honeybees and is good for the soil, since its roots fix nitrogen from the air.

There is a flower that Bees prefer -
And Butterflies - desire -
To gain the Purple Democrat
The Humming Bird - aspire -

And Whatsoever Insect pass -
A Honey bear away
Proportioned to his several dearth
And her - capacity -

Her face be rounder than the Moon
And ruddier than the Gown
Of Orchis in the Pasture -
Or Rhododendron - worn -

She doth not wait for June -
Before the World be Green -
Her sturdy little Countenance
Against the Wind - be seen -

Contending with the Grass -
Near Kinsman to Herself -
For privilege of Sod and Sun -
Sweet Litigants for Life -

And when the Hills be full -
And newer fashions blow -
Doth not retract a single spice
For pang of jealousy -

Her Public - be the Noon -
Her Providence - the Sun -
Her Progress - by the Bee - proclaimed -
In sovreign - Swerveless Tune -
The Bravest - of the Host -
Surrendering - the last -
Nor even of Defeat - aware -
When cancelled by the Frost -

(642)

With midsummer yawning ahead in Amherst, the frost is still far off. In the meadow, the woods, and the flower beds, Emily the gardener is in the midst of summer abundance. But in spite of this, it is the gardener's instinct to make more plants.

An Early Summer Garden Primer

A gardener wears many hats, and one of Emily's was a propagator's. Creating progeny of the pinks, she rooted cuttings, planted seeds, or took a division of the roots. Shoots put out roots; seeds split with a tendril descending, a nodding stem straightens.

Seed Starting 101

The most common way to make more plants in the garden and in nature is planting seeds. By planting seeds in a garden, we are actors in the great evolutionary imperative of the plant kingdom. The simple act of planting a seed brings life from dormancy. Emily noted "How few suggestions germinate," [24] but seeds are simpler than suggestions.

If you're sowing seeds outside, cultivate the soil to remove the weeds and aerate, helping water and air to penetrate. Make a shallow furrow, say half an inch deep, in a straight line if you're planting in rows or in a rounded shape if you are planting in sweeps. I use a hoe with a small, pointed blade, called a Cape Cod weeder, to prepare my seedbed. Read the seed packet. It will tell you how deep to plant. As a rule of thumb, cover the seed with soil equal to the diameter of the seed. Pat down the soil with your hands or the back of a tool. This helps the seed and soil make contact. Add water—a fine spray from a watering can or a hose, and the seed is ready for metaphor.

Longing is like the Seed
That wrestles in the Ground,
Believing if it intercede
It shall at length be found.

The Hour and the Clime -
Each circumstance unknown -
What Constancy must be achieved
Before it see the Sun!

(1298A)

In a few days or weeks, depending on the plant, small round seed leaves will emerge. Keep the soil gently watered. The new seedling consumes food from the seed itself, a literal root cellar, until photosynthesis gets started. If your seedlings are crowded, now is the time to thin them—snipping off or moving any extras to make room for each seedling to develop into a plant. It seems a bit cruel, but is important for healthy, well-blooming plants. Once again, the seed packet is a good reference for how far apart to space the growing plants.

Her propagation efforts weren't always successful. A friend sent her a cutting of a flowering plant from Florida. Emily later confessed to her, "The beautiful blossoms waned at last, the charm of all who knew them, resisting the effort of earth or air to persuade them to root, as the great florist says, 'The flower that never will in other climate grow.'" [25] The quote that Emily uses is from *Paradise Lost*.

Taking Root

Vegetative propagation—rooting a stem—is reproduction, creating two where there was one, like the story of Adam's rib. But it doesn't take divine intervention.

Find a shallow container with drainage holes. Anything will do—even a recycled plastic tub from the delicatessen. Fill the container with moist, sterilized potting soil or vermiculite.

Choose your target plant and cut a stem just below a set of leaves. Strip the leaves off near the cut; you'll see a slight swelling, called a "node." The node is the spot where the roots will emerge. Stick the stem into your container so that the node is under the soil, and firm the soil around it. Take a few cuttings and put them in the same container, just in case some don't root.

Label the container with a date and the type of cutting—it's amazing how easy it is to forget. Mist the cuttings and soil with a light spray of water and cover the container with plastic wrap to keep the humidity in. The plastic wrap shouldn't rest on the cuttings, so put stakes in the container to support it if necessary. The trick is to keep the cuttings moist, but not drenched, so check them occasionally.

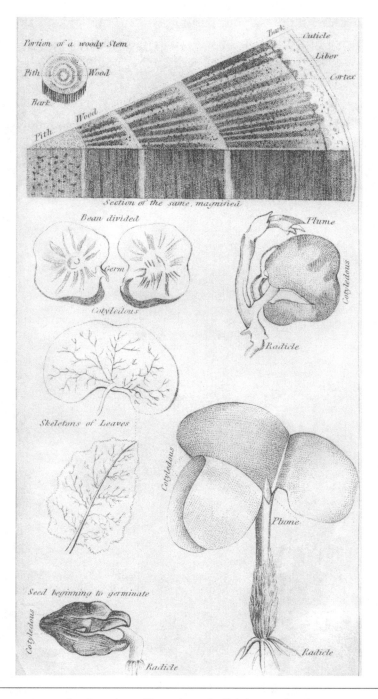

Seeds and seedlings, from Emily's botany book

In a month or less, your cuttings will start to look perky. If you give them a little tug, you'll feel some resistance. That means they've developed root systems and are ready to be "potted up"—planted in small individual pots.

You may wonder, "Can't you just root stems in water?" Everyone remembers a mother or teacher rooting coleus or philodendron in a glass on the windowsill. *Yes* is the answer, but the root systems will not be as vigorous or easy to transplant as cuttings grown in potting soil. Try it in soil—it's easy.

4

LATE SUMMER

A Gardener's Ground

*I*t is a sultry day, like a premonition. The air in her garden is thick, and as she walks among her borders, Emily muses, "The weather is like Africa and the Flowers like Asia."[1] Things are not only exotic, they've gotten a bit out of hand. There is mayhem in the border by late summer. It's crawling with nasturtiums. Heliotropes and marigolds bask in the hot sun. Baby's breath exhales, a white haze above the rest of the garden. Breathlessly, Emily sighs, "I've got a Geranium like a Sultana - and when the Humming birds come down - Geranium and I shut our eyes - and go far away."[2]

In the damp areas of the Dickinson meadow, the cardinal flowers are blooming a luscious jewel red. In the wooded areas around the house, the spring ephemeral wildflowers have disappeared, leaves and all. They withdraw in an early dormancy, fugitives from the summer heat.

By her late thirties, Emily also withdrew. No one is entirely sure why. It was gradual; if she were a celebrity, you would say she cancelled her public appearances. Rather than thinking of her as solitary, perhaps a better word would be "homebody," since she still saw a steady stream of family and friends at home. She called herself "a Balboa of house and garden."[3] A garden is a safe harbor for a landlocked Balboa. Plants are accepting of eccentricities.

I hav'nt told my garden yet -
Lest that should conquer me.
I hav'nt quite the strength now
To break it to the Bee -

I will not name it in the street
For shops w'd stare at me -
That one so shy - so ignorant
Should have the face to die.

The hillsides must not know it -
Where I have rambled so -
Nor tell the loving forests
The day that I shall go -

Nor lisp it at the table -
Nor heedless by the way
Hint that within the Riddle
One will walk today -

(40)

She wrote to a gentleman she was hoping to meet in 1869 that she would have to decline his invitation to a literary soiree in Boston. "Could it please your convenience to come so far as Amherst I should be very glad," she wrote him, "but I do not cross my Father's ground for any House or town."[4]

The Daylily Introduction

Her correspondent was Thomas Wentworth Higginson, a key player in
the Emily Dickinson chronicles. He was quite the Renaissance man: a
Unitarian minister, an anti-slavery and women's-rights activist, and a
regular feature writer for the *Atlantic Monthly*. He wrote about an array
of topics: nature, flowers, and in April 1862, an essay entitled "Letter to
a Young Contributor," giving advice to unpublished authors. This selec-
tion provoked an unusual response for Emily. She wrote him a letter
enclosing four of her poems. She opened, "Are you too deeply occupied
to say if my Verse is alive?" [5] It was the first of seventy-one letters she
sent him over the course of her lifetime. As she had hoped, he became
her mentor, her "Preceptor," as she would come to call him.

Higginson did find time to go as far as Amherst in 1870, eight years
after her first letter. On a warm Tuesday afternoon in August, he waited
for Emily in the front parlor. He described the Dickinson Homestead
to his wife this way: "A large county lawyer's house, brown brick, with
great trees & a garden—I sent up my card. A parlor dark & cool & stiff-
ish, a few books & engravings & an open piano." [6]

He described Emily's reddish hair and plain face, and her simple
dress of "exquisitely clean white pique & a blue net worsted shawl." Her
opening gambit was striking. "She came to me with two day lilies which
she put in a sort of childlike way into my hand & said, 'These are my
introduction.'" They had a long conversation, and he came back to the
house that evening for a closing call. He ended the letter to his wife that
night saying, "I never was with any one who drained my nerve power so
much." [7]

While Emily seemed to have no problem talking to Higginson,
she later wrote to him saying, "I am from the fields, you know, and while
quite at home with the Dandelion, make but sorry figure in a Drawing-
room." [8] She seemed to enjoy assuming a fairy-like existence, still wan-
dering the Dickinson meadow with her dog Carlo, but avoiding chance
encounters. "Of 'shunning Men and Women' - they talk of Hallowed

❧ HOSTA "EMILY DICKINSON" ❧

Daylily in bloom in mid-August? The ones I know are completely spent by late summer. In the mid-nineteenth century, the common name "day-lily" was the moniker for two plants: what we call "hosta" and what we call "daylily," *Hosta* and *Hemerocallis* for those of you who want the official names.

Hosta flowers are sweet-smelling, blooming on their curved or upright stems, lavender and white in the cool shade. As a plant, they are a tough customer, faithfully spreading, putting out their heart-shaped leaves in clumps and throwing up flower scapes year after year in late summer. *Hemerocallis* in Emily's day were orange and yellow. The individual blooms are larger and bright. The leaves are strappy. You decide.

In 1987, two hosta breeders, William and Eleanor Lachman, christened the result of a new cross in honor of Emily. The Lachmans were longtime Amherst residents and hybridizing hobbyists of the most serious sort.

The plant they named for Emily is a cross between the fragrant, old-fashioned species *Hosta plantaginea* and one of the jazzy new hybrids called "Neat Splash." The result is a compact plant, fairly restrained in comparison with some of the showgirls of the hosta world. It is medium-sized and a vigorous grower, standing about twenty inches tall with variegated leaves, green and white—a nod to the white dresses that Emily took to wearing constantly in her later years. It grows today in the gardens at the Dickinson Homestead.

Could this be the daylily of which Higginson wrote?

things, aloud - and embarrass my Dog - He and I dont object to them, if they'll exist their side." [9]

"The Little Garden Within"

Besides walking and gardening on the acres that comprised her father's grounds, she gardened inside the house. When Edward Dickinson started remodeling the brick mansion, he added a trendy conservatory. This glass room became Emily's domain, a place for her to cultivate plants year-round.

Emily's conservatory was a miniature, simplified version of the palm houses that were beginning to spring up all over England and

---

ᐅ A FLORAL LEXICON ᐊ

Emily once wrote, "Let me thank the little Cousin in flowers, which without lips, have language -"[10] The "language of flowers," in which special meanings were assigned to specific types of flowers, was in vogue during Emily's time. It originated in the European courts in the eighteenth century, where protocol was king—or queen, depending on the monarch. And it proliferated in the nineteenth century, seeding itself profusely across England and America as the romantic fever spread.

Some of the "words" in the language were obvious, like a forget-me-not symbolizing "keepsake." Others were more obscure, like marigolds standing in for grief. It was important to have the same dictionary if you were exchanging floral messages with a friend. In one translation, a daylily means "flirt"; in another it means "beauty." It seems unlikely that Emily was signaling coquetry to the married and just-introduced Thomas Wentworth Higginson. But beauty? Perhaps.

America. It was built on the southeast corner of the house. She called it her garden off the dining room. With the dining room windows open, heat drifted into the conservatory from the open Franklin stove. Emily stepped into her greenhouse room from a door in her father's study. Mullioned floor-to-ceiling windows, three to the south, one to the east, provided light and heat. White shelves lined the walls. There was prob-

Emily's conservatory, her "garden off the dining room"

ably a small potting bench or table to make it easier to work there. A door opened out for easy access to the garden.

Like many good Victorians, Emily was a magpie when it came to collecting plants. Exotic plants found their way to her conservatory— the booty of plant explorers who crossed oceans, climbed peaks, and negotiated dank jungles to bring back new species. Households in the Dickinsons' social strata collected specimens. It was a barometer of status: a blooming conservatory demonstrated the money to acquire plants and the leisure to sustain the bloom.

Home conservatories like Emily's were lush with plants. Flowering plants were favorites: begonias, jasmines, primroses, fuchsias, oleander, heliotropes, and pinks. Thrifty Yankee gardeners like Emily dug up plants from their flower borders or from the local woods and brought them inside.

Ferns were another favorite. Their fiddleheads and fronds appealed to an interest in texture. But Victorian gardeners also bought plants from catalogues: cactus, for example. Mattie tells us, "She tolerated none of the usual variety of mongrel house plants. A rare scarlet lily, a resurrection calla, perhaps—and here it was always summer with the oxalis dripping from hanging baskets like humble incense upon the heads of the household and its frequenters." [11]

Emily described her indoor bloom in one letter to her cousins, "Crocuses come up, in the garden off the dining room ... and a fuchsia, that pussy partook, mistaking it for strawberries. And that we have primroses - like the little pattern sent in last winter's note - and heliotropes by the aprons full, the mountain colored one - and a Jessamine bud, you know the little odor like Lubin, - and gillyflowers, magenta, and few mignonette and sweet alyssum bountiful, and carnation buds." [12] Because of their cool temperatures, conservatories were great venues for forcing bulbs like crocus.

The microclimate of a well-situated conservatory gives the gardener better odds at bringing plants into flower off-season. The bright light and concentrated heat from the sun in Emily's south-facing conservatory signaled plants to bloom. Sharing some of her conservatory

flowers, she once wrote, "I send you inland buttercups as out-door flow-
ers are still at sea." [13] One of her poems has a sort of itemization of plants
in her conservatory.

I tend my flowers for thee -
Bright Absentee!
My Fuschzia's Coral Seams
Rip - while the Sower - dreams -

Geraniums - tint - and spot -
Low Daisies - dot -
My Cactus - splits her Beard
To show her throat -

Carnations - tip their spice -
And Bees - pick up -
A Hyacinth - I hid -
Puts out a Ruffled Head -
And odors fall
From flasks - so small -
You marvel how they held -

Globe Roses - break their satin flake -
Opon my Garden floor -
Yet - thou - not there -
I had as lief they bore
No crimson - more -

(367)

A conservatory creates an ongoing round of work, a pleasant but
steady stream of chores. Plants require tending: trimming, turning, pot-
ting up. They dry out quickly in clay pots, and Emily would have car-

ried in water from the pump in the kitchen. The trick in a conservatory, or in any garden for that matter, is to water each plant to its needs. Gardeners create a strange world of jungle and desert. Ferns demand moisture; cacti need drought. Emily sometimes got the watering done with a Tom Sawyer technique. Her niece described it this way: "She let me water her plants in her little conservatory—cape jasmine, heliotrope, and ferns—reaching up to the higher shelves by a tiny watering-pot with a long, slender spout like the antennae of insects, which had been made for her after an idea of her father's." [14]

Emily invited other innocents to join her in her indoor garden. You can almost hear her calling out to a little neighborhood boy, MacGregor Jenkins, from the conservatory door. "'Come quickly,' she said, 'if you want to see something beautiful.' [He] followed her and she pointed out a wonderful moth which had broken its chrysalis and was fluttering about the flowers." [15] We'll never know if she found the chrysalis on her father's grounds or if someone brought it to her.

In the conservatory as well as in the garden, Emily was partial to place names, collecting the romantic and exotic, the Orient and the Sahara among others. She linked these places to her indoor bloom. "My flowers are near and foreign," she told a friend, "and I have but to cross the floor to stand in the Spice Isles. The wind blows gay today and the Jays bark like Blue Terriers." [16]

A Little Catalogue of Emily's Conservatory Plants

CAPE JASMINE (*Gardenia jasminoides veitchii*) Emily sent a bloom of cape jasmine, what we would call gardenia, to a friend to mark a special occasion. Her niece called it "her crowning attention." [17] Gardenias are those fickle plants with shiny leaves and sultry perfumed white blossoms. When you buy them, they're always healthy, blooming, and straight out of the greenhouse. When they arrive home, they generally pitch a fit—leaves yellow and buds drop. Their needs are many.

⤙ TIP ⤚

Gardenias like acid soil, so feed them regularly with an acidifying fertilizer like Miracid, following the directions on the box. If white crusty minerals build up around the top of the pot, water monthly with distilled water. Like a lady protecting her complexion, gardenias like to be perfectly positioned in at least four hours a day of filtered, indirect sunlight. And to set buds, they need temperatures around sixty degrees at night, seventy during the day. Spider mites love to set up residence in their foliage, so spray them often with a direct blast of water. And did I mention humidity? Gardenias are jungle plants and expect a rainforest atmosphere. Mist them several times a day, or set their pots in a tray filled with gravel that has water in it.

FUCHSIA (*Fuchsia hybrida*) Who put the Fuchs in fuchsia? The plant that Emily grew was named for Leonhart Fuchs, a sixteenth-century German medical professor who first described it botanically. It hails from New Zealand and South America. Pink, red, and purple bells hang down, making it a great choice to drape over the edge of a conservatory shelf or cascade over a hanging basket. It benefits from pinching and pruning, so one of Emily's tasks every year was to give the fuchsia a haircut—unless one of Vinnie's cats was around to eat it. If fuchsia isn't pruned it gets leggy and out of shape.

Fuchsia "that pussy partook"

⊰ **TIP** ⊱

If you are growing fuchsia yourself, cut back on watering in the early winter, then around Valentine's Day give it more water and some fertilizer. That should make it burst into bloom. In summer, give it some shade and some space, because it likes good air circulation.

OLEANDER (*Nerium oleander*) If Emily had written murder mysteries, this plant could have been featured prominently, since all parts are poisonous. Even smoke from burning the plant can be toxic. But if you ignore its weapons-grade aspects and can avoid ingesting it, oleander is a lovely greenhouse plant. Its leaves are glossy and evergreen. Its flowers cluster at the ends of its stems and are generally pink, though they're now available in many colors thanks to the hybridizer's magic touch.

DAPHNE (*Daphne odora*) On the occasion of Thomas Wentworth Higginson's second visit to the Dickinson Homestead in 1873, Emily greeted him with another flower. Instead of an August "daylily," she glided in with a bloom of daphne. Daphne is an evergreen shrub, and is known for being a bit finicky. It wants just the right amount of shade and moisture, not too much and not too little. As you might expect from its odoriferous ephithet, daphne is prized for its fragrance. This particular species isn't hardy as far north as Amherst, so we know that Emily grew it indoors.

The Gardening Sisters

While the conservatory was Emily's province, she did share it. "Vinnie is happy with her duties, her pussies, and her posies, for the little gar-

Vinnie

den within, though tiny, is triumphant. There are scarlet carnations, with a witching suggestion, and hyacinths covered with promises which I know they will keep." [18]

Emily and Vinnie shared the outdoor garden as well. It sounds as though they were a bit like the odd couple, gardening-wise, since Vinnie believed in a sort of laissez-faire approach. Mattie tells us that "all the flowers did as they liked: tyrannized over her, hopped out of their own beds into each other's beds, were never reproved or removed as long as they bloomed; for a live flower to Aunt Lavinia was more than any dead horticultural principle." [19]

Vinnie was only one of Emily's gardening sisters. In an early poem, Emily wrote, "One Sister have I in our house - and one a hedge away." [20] The sister on the other side of the hedge was her sister-in-law, Susan Gilbert Dickinson. Looking out of her bedroom window on the west side of the house, Emily could see the Evergreens, their elaborate house next door.

Before Susan and Austin married in 1856, Edward Dickinson made them an offer the couple couldn't refuse: a new house built in a style of their choice on the substantial lot next door and a partnership in his law practice for Austin. The couple set out to make a showplace. The architecture of their "cottage" was the then-trendy villa style called Italianate. In its square tower, they could survey the Amherst landscape and get a bird's-eye view of their own garden. Even the name that they gave the house, the Evergreens, reflected their gardening interests. How the neighbors must have gossiped to see this outlandish house and garden emerge for the Dickinson heir apparent and his ambitious bride.

The path between the houses was well-trod, and Emily was a frequent visitor to the Evergreens. "It was here that she would fly to the piano, if the mood required, and thunder out a composition of her own which she laughingly but appropriately called 'The Devil,'" one contemporary remembered. She visited day and night. "When her father came, lantern in hand, to see that she reached home in safety, she would elude him and dart through the darkness to reach home before him." [21]

Austin and the Fine Art of Landscape Gardening

Gardens are subject to fashion. A stroll around the Evergreens was a walk through a landscape patterned in the latest mid-century cuts. It almost swoons, it is so romantic. Stone steps and two stone terraces lead up to the front door, with masses of rhododendron and English hawthorn. Beds are curved, shrubbery is massed, and views are composed to be visually pleasing from the doors, windows, and gates.

On the west side of the house, Austin and Susan designed their "piazza" around an ancient apple tree, leaving an opening in the roof for its gnarled branches. A vine clambers up to drape the edge with bloom and greenery. On the lawn, another apple tree is transformed into a living summer house. Its built-in seat is six feet above the ground, reachable by a set of wooden stairs. There are garden benches set in the lawn, adding interest and shady rest stops.

This romantic landscaping was a backlash against American-style gardening, those tidy symmetrical flower beds that colonists laid out as soon as they hacked their way out of the wilderness. With the forest looming around them, it's small wonder that our forefathers and foremothers wanted to see nice right angles, an imposed formality to give them some sense of control. Even the gardens at the Homestead with their combination of flower beds and vegetable rows were a remnant of that formal style.

Austin spent much of his spare time in the garden and was something of a horticultural sophisticate. He planted a bank of rhododendron to flank the Evergreens library and collected ferns on his outings. One that still grows on the south side of the Evergreens is the royal fern (*Osmunda regalis*). A stately monarch of the fern world, its fronds can grow to three feet. It couldn't have gotten there on its own, since you would only find it in swampy terrain. Still, it—like much of nature— is tolerant of change, and happily adapted to its new home on the Dickinson property.

Austin and Sue were well connected, and enjoyed entertaining in their new home. He especially enjoyed having guests at bloom time for

The Evergreens

the rhododendron and magnolias. His guests included Frederick Law Olmsted and Calvert Vaux, the partners who are famous, and were already well known then, for designing New York's Central Park. Both men ate many times at Sue's table—Vaux gave her one of his books, *Villas and Cottages*, and inscribed it to her. Of their visits, Mattie reminisced that, "once during a twilight supper, discussing the peculiarities of a certain blue spruce, the men with one accord left the table to examine it at the extreme end of the grounds, returning twenty minutes later, still completely absorbed in their subject, and quite regardless of the hiatus in the meal."[22] You can still see a blue spruce on the eastern end of the property, overgrown and stressed by faster-growing competition that has caused it to lose its lower limbs.

Following another horticultural trend, Austin imported unusual varieties of trees to the Evergreens. Gentlemen of a certain social standing enjoyed creating arboreta.

A Little Catalogue of Austin's Specimen Trees

Three unusual trees still shade the Evergreens property:

A female gingko tree

GINGKO (*Gingko biloba*) On the west side of the Evergreens, a gingko tree casts its unusual shadow. Each leaf is shaped like a small, elegant fan, with a notch in the center making two lobes: thus, *bi-loba*. In autumn, the leaves turn to solid gold and drop in one day, making a yellow carpet under the tree. After the leaves drop, the tree has an especially distinctive look. The leaves are carried on woody spurs that stick out from the branches, and the profile of the leafless tree is a bit gawky, almost as if it's had a bad hair day. While Austin didn't know this at the time he planted it, the gingko is a particularly tough tree, withstanding poor soil, drought, and air pollution. So it has turned into a popular city tree. Unlike most trees, gingkos are separately sexed; *dioecious* is the botany class term. Be sure you get a male. The fruit-bearing females have earned the nickname "stink-o gingko," because their ripening fruits have an almost indescribably foul odor.

UMBRELLA TREE (*Magnolia tripelata*) Walking around the property at the Evergreens in midsummer, you will see trees with huge leaves and smooth grey bark. If you get caught in a summer shower, you'll see how they earned the sobriquet "umbrella tree." Native to the mid-Atlantic and points south, this relative of the southern magnolia is tougher, able to withstand colder climes. It's a prolific self-sower, as evidenced by the many seedlings that still grow around the property and beyond. Mattie, as an adult, gave one of its offspring to a friend, Mrs. Arthur Dakin, who lived on South Pleasant Street; that seedling now shades the Dakin house. Its large leaves are matched by showy white flowers and equally showy red fall fruits.

JAPANESE TREE LILAC (*Syringa reticulata*) This is a tree that will stump your horticultural friends. An actual lilac, it grows as a small tree with a single trunk rather than as the usual clumpy shrub. And it blooms in June with yellowish-white flowers, at least a month after you've deadheaded the old-fashioned lilacs. It has no pests or diseases, not even the powdery mildew that plagues its cousins. Unfortunately, in what seems to be a karmic tradeoff, it lacks that intoxicating lilac scent.

Sister Sue's Gardens

With Austin's trees it was, by all accounts, a beautiful property. Edward Dickinson's bargain with his son had paid off. Susan quickly left her mark on the gardens too.

Sue loved her flowers. A rose called "Baltimore Belle" stretched out its canes with fragrant clusters of light pink every June. She underplanted the rose with purple heliotrope and the soft grey leaves of scented geranium. Mattie sometime collected tiny bunches of flowers and made buttonhole bouquets for her parents' guests.

With a backdrop of conifers, Sue planted a huge skyline of hollyhocks along the path to her in-laws' house. By late summer they were taller than Emily, with wide single flowers opening along the stalks from the bottom up. Children like to make dolls out of the blooms—turned upside down each bloom looks like a lovely wide skirt and the buds look like heads. Hollyhocks drop their skirts when they are finished blooming. "I am very busy picking up stems and stamens as the hollyhocks leave their clothes around," Emily once wryly noted.[23]

The Little Ones

One of Emily's joys was the presence of her niece and nephews next door. After the first was born, Emily wrote to a friend, "Sue - draws her little Boy - pleasant days - in a Cab - and Carlo walks behind, accompanied by a Cat - from each Establishment - It looks funny to see so small a man, going out of Austin's House -"[24] Children's voices now animated the gardens around the Evergreens and the Homestead.

Austin and Sue had three children: Edward, Martha, and Gilbert, called Ned, Mattie, and Gib respectively. They were a rambunctious crew, and Emily loved them dearly. Ned pilfered from other people's orchards. "We have all heard of the Boy whose Constitution required stolen fruit," Emily wrote to him, "though his Father's Orchard was loaded - There was something in the unlawfulness that gave it a saving flavor."[25] Mattie skipped church and spent her time with Aunt Emily in the conservatory or the garden. Gib stopped by and asked for a plant to bring to his teacher, but Aunt Emily was asleep. When she woke up, she brought over a plant with a note for him. "Aunt Emily waked up now, and brought this little Plant all the way from her Crib for Gilbert to carry to his Teacher - Good Night - Aunt Emily's asleep again." [26]

Messages passed back and forth regularly between the houses. Timothy, the hired hand, walked the foaming pails of milk from the Homestead's cows to the Evergreens. The three children watched his approach in anticipation until their mother released them to run and see if Aunt Emily had sent anything along. Mattie remembered fondly, "Oftenest it was a cardboard box, and Tim said, as we took it from him, 'From Miss Im'ly.' In it would be perhaps three tiny frosted, heart-shaped cakes, or some of her chocolate caramels—with a flower on top, heliotrope, a red lily, or cape jasmine—and underneath always a note or a poem for our mother." [27]

The neighborhood children joined the Dickinsons, playing on the property around both houses. In later life, they reminisced about the romantic possibilities of the garden, orchard, and outbuildings, perfect settings for gypsy camps or pirate adventures. They all knew Miss Emily. "She was not shy with them. She was a splendid comrade and a staunch companion. Her ready smile, her dancing eyes, her quick reply made us all tingle with pleasure when we were near her." [28]

Emily knew how to entertain the gang. In a designated post office in the hedge, she traded secret messages with the sometimes pirates, sometimes gypsies. She would lower gingerbread in a basket from her bedroom window. They would put in a daisy or clover in return. "We knew the things she loved best and we sought the early wild flowers, a flaming leaf, a glistening stone, the shining, fallen feather of a bird and took them to her, sure of her appreciation of the gift as well as the giving." [29] So if Emily had given up her wildflower wanderings, she still had her emissaries to bring her plunder.

She must have been an interesting puzzle to them. "She had a habit of standing in rapt attention as if she were listening to something very faint and far off. We children often saw her at sunset, standing at the kitchen window, peering through a vista in the trees to the western sky,—her proud little head thrown back, her eyes raised and one hand held characteristically before her." ³⁰ To some of the little girls in the Dickinson set, she wrote a special gardening fable:

> *Little Women*
> *Which shall it be, Geraniums or Tulips?*
> *The butterfly up in the sky that hasn't any name*
> *And hasn't any tax to pay and hasn't any home*
> *Is just as high as you and I, and higher, I believe*
> *So soar away and never sigh*
> *For that's the way to grieve.*³¹

It was summer; long days stretched to sunset, butterflies meandered, and geraniums—not tulips—bloomed in Emily's garden.

Late Summer in Emily Dickinson's Garden

"Old Testament weather." ³²

The heat in the garden has its own presence. In August, the thermometer often lurks near ninety, and it is so humid that the air seems to slow everything down. These are the dog days, so named for the rising of Sirius, the Dog Star, under whose influence the heat is supposed to wag its tail or hang out its tongue. Emily seemed to enjoy it, though the garden and her sister may not have. "The Days are very hot and the Weeds pant like the centre of Summer. They say the Corn likes it. I thought there were others besides the Corn. How deeply I was deluded! Vinnie rocks her Garden and moans that God wont help her." ³³

A dry spell is not uncommon and Emily makes the best of it, plumbing the climate for a good turn of phrase. "We are reveling in a gorgeous drought," she wrote. "The grass is painted brown, and how nature would look in other than the standard colors, we can all infer." ³⁴

As a gardener and a poet, she seemed to accept weather extremes. Another day she noted, "Today is parched and handsome, though the Grass is the color of Statesmen's Shoes, and only the Butterfly rises to the situation."[35] No one can call Emily a fair-weather gardener.

It's time to water in the garden. In the days before sprinkler systems and soaker hoses, Emily watered the old-fashioned way, filling a pail or watering can. One August, Emily reported, "Vinnie is trading with a Tin peddler - buying Water pots for me to sprinkle Geraniums with."[36] A Victorian aerobic exercise, she filled them from a well or a pump; we know there was at least one out back near the barn.

What mystery pervades a well!
The water lives so far -
A neighbor from another world
Residing in a jar

Whose limit none have ever seen,
But just his lid of glass -
Like looking every time you please
In an abyss's face!

The grass does not appear afraid,
I often wonder he
Can stand so close and look so bold
At what is awe to me.

Related somehow they may be,
The sedge stands next the sea
Where he is floorless
And does no timidity betray -

A water pot to sprinkle the geraniums

But nature is a stranger yet;
The ones that cite her most
Have never passed her haunted house,
Nor simplified her ghost.

To pity those that know her not
Is helped by the regret
That those who know her, know her less
The nearer her they get.

(1433A)

Mosquitoes whine, zeroing in on the gardener's exposed skin. Wrists and ankles make particular targets, even in those days when sleeves and skirts covered more of the gardener. Suntans were not in fashion, so a gardening hat was a required part of the costume.

Summer laid her simple Hat
On its boundless shelf -
Unobserved - a Ribin slipt,
Snatch it for yourself.

Summer laid her supple Glove
In its sylvan Drawer -
Wheresoe'er, or was she -
The demand of Awe?

(1411D, 1411E)

So in her cotton dress, Emily would don a gardening bonnet and go out to work in her summer garden. She was pleased with her flowers and the relatively few demands they made.

❧

They ask but our Delight -
The Darlings of the Soil
And grant us all their Countenance
For a penurious smile -

(908)

Leaves on the trees are heavy, almost tired, the dark green of summer forgetting the spring chartreuse. Late in the day Emily feels a shift in the direction of the wind. The sky darkens with accumulating nimbus and the change in air pressure makes the leaves blow upside down.

⊰ OFF WITH THEIR HEADS ⊱

Besides watering, one of the most important summer chores in Emily's garden was deadheading. Many perennials and most annuals will set seeds if the flower blossoms mature. They're doing what comes naturally, producing more offspring. As gardeners, we exercise the power: will it be more flowers, or is it seed-setting time?

To deadhead, simply clip off the spent bloom with scissors or your fingers, but learn where and when the next flower bud pops out. Some plants throw out new flower stalks only basally, from the bottom of the plant where it intersects with the roots. Other plants create side shoots that make their appearance from the leaf axils.

Use care when deadheading plants like lilies. Their brittle buds are formed in clusters that open almost reluctantly, one or two at a time. If you are too enthusiastic at deadheading time, you can break off the unopened buds.

The Leaves like Women, interchange
Sagacious Confidence -
Somewhat of Nods and somewhat
Portentous inference -

The Parties in both cases
Enjoining secrecy -
Inviolable compact
To notoriety.

(1098B)

Her skin tingles with the approach of the storm as she moves inside to
watch the fireworks: thunder and lightning and with luck, a downpour,
a labor-free watering for the garden, washing off the dust.

The Wind begun to rock the Grass
With threatening Tunes and low -
He threw a Menace at the Earth -
A Menace at the Sky -

The Leaves unhooked themselves from Trees -
And started all abroad
The Dust did scoop itself like Hands
And throw away the Road.

The Wagons quickened on the Streets
The Thunders hurried slow -
The Lightning showed a Yellow Beak
And then a livid Claw -

The Birds put up the Bars to Nests -
The Cattle flung to Barns -
There came one drop of Giant Rain
And then as if the Hands

That held the Dams had parted hold
The Waters wrecked the Sky -
But overlooked my Father's House -
Just quartering a Tree -

(796C)

From the front windows of the Homestead, Emily looked out onto a hedge and a substantial picket fence. This elegant wooden barrier was the descendent of simple palings, sharpened saplings stuck into the ground to make a barrier. New England farmers used them first to keep animals in a pen, or out of a garden. A later Amherst poet, Robert Frost, made the saying "Good fences make good neighbors" famous, and the Dickinsons wanted everyone to know that they were good and prosperous neighbors. A fence marks the edge of a garden or property, and provides an enclosure, like an arm wrapped around a friend.

In front of the Homestead, the fence had three gates: two for people and one for carriages. It extended to the Evergreens property. To leave a gate open was a misdemeanor in Edward Dickinson's book, and Austin picked up the idea from his father. A neighborhood boy often forgot to shut it. "If this happened, I was almost certain to hear a stentorian voice in the distance saying in accents none too mild, 'Boy, shut that gate.' It was Austin Dickinson in the garden or on the piazza who had observed me and the open gate." [37]

The Dickinsons planted the first hemlock hedge surrounding the Evergreens and the Homestead in the spring of 1865. Emily, visiting Fanny and Loo in Cambridge, wrote to Vinnie, "I hope the Chimneys are done and the Hemlocks set, and the Two Teeth filled, in the Front yard - How astonishing it will be to me." [38] The "two teeth" were most likely the ornamental gateposts, and the picket fence and its gates were installed at the same time.

Setting a hedge is an event. You can imagine Edward directing the hired men. They would have hammered posts in the ground and run a string between them to be sure that the plants would go in along a straight line. A stash of small hemlocks would have been corralled somewhere on the property, waiting for their new home.

Hemlock (*Tsuga canadensis*) was an excellent choice. It is native to the Amherst area, growing in the woods in shaded areas. Thus when needed for a hedge, it will grow happily under the canopy of larger trees, such as oaks. It also, in gardener's lingo, "takes pruning." In short, it can be shaped by shearing, which not only keeps it to size, but also gives it shape by encouraging the tips to branch out. It is evergreen and looks as good in the winter as it does in the summer.

    ◞

I think the Hemlock likes to stand
Opon a Marge of Snow -
It suits his own Austerity -
And satisfies an awe

That men, must slake in Wilderness -
And in the Desert - cloy -
An instinct for the Hoar, the Bald -
Lapland's - nescessity -

The Hemlock's nature thrives - on cold -
The Gnash of Northern winds
Is sweetest nutriment - to him -
His best Norwegian Wines -

To satin Races - he is nought -
But children on the Don,
Beneath his Tabernacles, play,
And Dnieper Wrestlers, run.

(400)

The hedge at the Homestead created a boundary and added curb appeal. It made a statement that this house was separate from the rest of the town, separate from the Boston road. Over time, it also added privacy.

A hedge is a large horizontal accent in the garden, offsetting the large verticals lent by the trees. It creates a green wall, a frame for the garden, a dark backdrop for more colorful plants. Emily noted the contrast the hedge provides to nature beyond.

A Lady red, amid the Hill
Her annual secret keeps.
A Lady white, within the field
In chintz and lily, sleeps.

The tidy Breezes, with their Brooms
Sweep Vale, and hill, and tree -
Prithee, my pretty Housewives!
Who may expected be?

The neighbors do not yet suspect!
The woods exchange a smile!
Orchard, and Buttercup, and Bird
In such a little while!

And yet how *still* the Landscape stands!
How nonchalant the Hedge!
As if the *Resurrection*
Were nothing very strange!

(137A)

Past the hedge across Main Street, the Dickinson meadow stretched down to the brook. Emily could see the brick factory with its smokestacks at a distance, busy manufacturing hats out of imported palm leaf. A child acquaintance wrote that the meadow ". . . was

HEDGE FUNDS

Spring and fall are good seasons to plant a hedge, allowing the plants to establish before the extremes of heat and cold. Emily's father planted their hedge in May. Dig a bed the length of the hedge, approximately eight inches deep by a foot wide. Remove any large rocks and incorporate compost to improve the quality of the soil.

For a sheared formal hedge like the Dickinsons', put in a plant every two to five feet, depending on the spread of the plants. Spread out the roots of the plants, and plant them at the level of the nursery soil. Once all of the plants are installed, clip them to an even height.

Water, and keep watering to help the plants get used to their new location. Give your hedge an inch of water a week during the growing season for the first year. If you're not sure how much that is, put an empty tuna can under your sprinkler or watering can and see how long it takes to fill up. Be sure to water especially well in the fall to give the plants the best shot for coming through the winter in good condition.

A hedge is a commitment. Unlike a fence, it doesn't require paint, but it does require pruning at least once a year. Turn your back for a few years, and you may find that your hedge has reverted into a closely planted line of tree monsters.

Good candidates for evergreen hedges are arborvitae and yew, if you don't have deer, or upright junipers and Leyland cypress if you do. Hemlock, like the Dickinsons planted, requires annual spraying with a horticultural oil to combat a chewy pest called the wooly adelgid. Both beech and hornbeam make lovely deciduous hedges, exposing their branch structures each winter. And there is always privet, a well-worn but dependable choice.

The Dickinson hedge was traditional, made of one type of plant. If you are planting a hedge in your own garden, you could also con-

continued ─────────────────────────────────────

sider a tapestry hedge made up of more than one kind of flowering shrub. By interweaving large plants with arching branches and bloom times, a tapestry hedge provides color interest as well as privacy. Good companions for a tapestry are lilac and forsythia, and old-fashioned favorites like mock orange, weigela, bridal wreath spiraea (*Spiraea van-houteii*) and beautybush (*Kolkwitzia amabilis*). Small flowering trees like crab apples add height to the hedge and are especially effective if the hedge turns a corner.

unbroken then by houses . . . The long grass was filled with clover and buttercups and Queen Anne's lace, all swaying in the breeze, a favorite haunt of bees and butterflies and bobolinks." [39] Emily herself was inspired to write:

To make a prairie it takes a clover and one bee,
One clover, and a bee,
And revery.
The revery alone will do,
If bees are few.

(1779)

The hay in the meadow was a crop, cut at least twice a year for the cows and horses in the barn. By August it was rowen grass, the second growth, recovered from mowing earlier in the season. It waved in the haze.

The Grass so little has to do,
A Sphere of simple Green -
With only Butterflies, to brood,
And Bees, to entertain -

And stir all day to pretty tunes
The Breezes fetch along,
And hold the Sunshine, in its lap
And bow to everything,

And thread the Dews, all night, like Pearl,
And make itself so fine
A Duchess, were too common
For such a noticing,

And even when it die, to pass
In odors so divine -
As lowly spices, gone to sleep -
Or Amulets of Pine -

And then to dwell in Sovreign Barns,
And dream the Days away,
The Grass so little has to do,
I wish I were a Hay -

(379B)

Whether the meadow was a haymow or a prairie, when the hay came into the barn, the nephews, niece, and their friends viewed it as an inalienable right to climb the ladder to the loft and fling themselves into the piles of sweet-smelling clover hay.

Going out of the kitchen door, Emily looked up to their "sovereign" barn. The barn was roomy enough to house tools, a grinding wheel, the horses, the cabriolet lined in yellow broadcloth, the sleigh, the milk cow, chickens, and a pig. The animals in turn provided the manure that enriched the garden.

By late summer, though, Emily would have wondered if her garden had ever needed fertilizer. Huge flowers towered over her, and vines clambered and climbed.

A Little Catalogue of Emily's Flowering Vines

Flowering vines are the acrobats of any summer garden, including Emily's, scaling heights with different schemes. Some use tendrils, transforming small parts of their leaves or stems to go the distance. Others perform their high-wire acts by twisting their entire stems, like boa constrictors or elephant's trunks. Still others, ivy for example, shoot out tenacious little roots, adventurers exploring crevices in bark or masonry.

NASTURTIUMS (*Tropaeolum majus*) Nasturtiums were Vinnie's favorites. They move along the ground or over any obstacle by way of twining petioles, leaf stalks.

CLEMATIS (*Clematis spp.*) Clematis is a vine with a three-part leaf and a curling frizzy seed. For reasons unknown, the pronunciation is

---

⊰ **TIP** ⊱

Sow nasturtiums directly outside, since they resent transplanting. Then ignore them. They don't like to be fed, so put away the fertilizer, and unless it is incredibly dry they don't even need much water. Their yellow, red, and orange blooms will reward you all summer for your negligence. As a bonus, they are entirely edible—flower, leaf, and stem.

The ways that vines climb, from Emily's botany book

clem'atis, with the emphasis on the first syllable. It appears in Emily's herbarium and in one of her poems:

'Tis Customary as we part
A Trinket - to confer -
It helps to stimulate the faith
When Lovers be afar -

'Tis various - as the various taste -
Clematis - journeying far -
Presents me with a single Curl
Of her Electric Hair -

(628)

⊰ TIP ⊱

Different types of clematis bloom at different times of year, but they are steady, reliable vines that climb with a modified leaf stalk that morphs into a tendril. Their roots appreciate some shade, so they are a great candidate for underplanting with a perennial like hosta or phlox. They'll even accept partial shade.

SWEET PEA (*Lathyrus latifolius*) Sweet peas curl their tendrils around any skinny support. They'll happily grasp a string or wire before shooting out more stems. Their blooms are pink, fragrant, and generous. "I write in the midst of Sweet-Peas and by the side of Orioles," Emily wrote, "and could put my Hand on a Butterfly, only he withdraws." [40] Grow them for the smell and as wonderful flowers to cut and bring inside. Emily exaggerated for effect, telling Fanny, "Loo left a tumbler of sweet-peas on the green room bureau," she said. "I am going to leave them there till they make pods and sow themselves in the upper drawer, and then I guess they'll blossom about Thanksgiving time." [41]

MORNING GLORY (*Ipomea purpurea*)   Morning glories open to trumpet in the day, a silent duet with the Dickinsons' rooster. The flowers open around dawn, so keep a farmer's schedule if you want to see them unfurl. "Such a purple morning," Emily wrote, "even to the morning-glory that climbs the cherry tree." [42] The stems twine, which is why it was also called *convolvulus*, like a convoluted sentence. The higher it climbs, the tighter it hugs the cherry tree or any vertical support. If you want to grow morning glories like Emily's, soak the seeds overnight and plant them in peat pots a month before the last frost. Then transplant them, pot and all, into the garden around Memorial Day.

Unlike sweet peas, morning glories aren't good for cutting. Emily spoofed Scottish poet Robert Burns in this ditty:

Poor little Heart!
Did they forget thee?
Then dinna care! Then dinna care!

Proud little Heart!
Did they forsake thee?
Be debonnaire! Be debonnaire!

Frail little Heart!
I would not break thee -
Could'st credit *me*? Could'st credit me?

Gay little Heart -
Like Morning Glory!
Wind and Sun - wilt thee array!

(214)

Color in Emily's Garden

Beyond morning glories, Emily liked purple in the garden. She once wrote that she was "grasping the proudest zinnia from my purple garden."[43] Her flower colors of choice were the cool end of the spectrum: pink and blue, purple and lavender, plus white for contrast. Thomas Wentworth Higginson lets us in on her palette in one of his letters to Emily: "I wish you could see some field lilies, yellow & scarlet, painted in water colors that are just sent to us for Christmas. These are not your favorite colors, & perhaps I love the azure & gold myself—but perhaps we should learn to love & cultivate these ruddy hues of life."[44]

So much about gardening is reminiscing. When Mattie once called her aunt's garden "a butterfly Utopia"[45] she was remembering late summer. Butterflies are sun worshippers, their bodies waiting to register temperatures in the mid- to upper eighties in order to fly. They came to Emily's garden because they live off of the nectar in flowers.

The butterflies also feed on nectar in the Dickinson meadow, on the butterfly weed that grows up among the grasses. But it's time to mow the hay again, and in late summer Emily would have heard the whine of blade against whetstone and have seen the hired men swinging their huge scythes, leaving swathes of mown grass like a wake from a boat. The wind brought the smell of cut grass up to Emily's window.

The Wind didn't come from the Orchard - today -
Further than that -
Nor stop to play with the Hay -
Nor threaten a Hat -
He's a transitive fellow - very -
Rely on that -

A swallowtail butterfly, its caterpillar, and its chrysalis

If He leave a Bur at the door
We know He has climbed a Fir -
But the Fir is Where - Declare -
Were you ever there?

If He bring Odors of Clovers -
And that is His business - not Ours -
Then He has been with the Mowers -
Whetting away the Hours
To sweet pauses of Hay -
His Way - of a June Day -

If He fling Sand, and Pebble -
Little Boy's Hats - and stubble -
With an occasional steeple -
And a hoarse "Get out of the Way, I say",
Who'd be the fool to stay?
Would you - Say -
Would you be the fool to stay?

(494B)

They turned the hay over in the coming days, encouraging it to
dry. One literally makes hay while the sun shines. Eventually the hay
was stacked, brought across Main Street, and forked into the top of
the barn.

Besides raising hay to feed the cows and horses, the Dickinsons
grew vegetables to extend their table. Describing the vegetable garden
at the North Pleasant Street house, Emily tells Austin, "The garden is
amazing - we have beets and beans, have had *splendid potatoes* for three
weeks now. Old Amos [the gardener] weeds and hoes and has oversight
of all thoughtless vegetables." [46]

The thoughtless vegetables at the Homestead occupied a large plot
flanking the flower garden, separated visually from it by the asparagus

bed. Asparagus stalks shot up from the roots in early spring, giving the Dickinsons a harvest that lasted more than a month. By foregoing the thinner stems, they allowed the bed to build up strength for the following year. Left to their own devices, those pencil-thin stems burst into a bank of rich ferny foliage. Emily cut them during the summer to decorate the Franklin stoves and fireplaces. Asparagus is a crossover plant, both functional and decorative, perfectly suited to divide the flowers from their productive, if pedestrian, neighbors.

By midsummer, the vegetable garden really starts to produce. Beyond the asparagus bed, pole beans are twining up stakes. Mattie describes them as "flaunted red and white, like country girls in gay calico." [47] These colorful climbers are scarlet runner beans. Mattie positions them "next to the superior lima variety in green satin, and tall corn with tempting tassels for young fingers." [48]

While flowers appear in force in Emily's poems, and fruit on occasion, vegetables rarely made it. But in one, Emily alludes to the fact that raising corn (or grapes) in New England soil wasn't easy.

On the Bleakness of my Lot
Bloom I strove to raise -
Late - my Garden of a Rock
Yielded Grape - and Maize -

   (862B)

Some days, out weeding in the summer heat, the gardener's lot can seem pretty bleak.

Like all good gardeners, the Dickinsons shared their yield with friends and family, and received in turn. Emily wrote to her cousin Louisa one summer, "I cooked the peaches as you told me, and they swelled to beautiful fleshy halves and tasted quite magic. The beans we fricasseed and they made a savory cream in cooking that 'Aunt Emily' (her mother) liked to sip. She was always fonder of julep food than of more substantial." [49] If plants really produce, they quickly exceed one family's ability to consume them.

In the center of summer, more berries bear. When she was young, Emily went berrying with friends and with Vinnie, picking raspberries and blackberries that grew in abundance in the hedgerows around town.

⌒⌒

Would you like Summer? Taste of ours -
Spices? Buy - here!
Ill! We have Berries, for the parching!
Weary! Furloughs of Down!
Perplexed! Estates of Violet - Trouble ne'er looked on!
Captive! We bring Reprieve of Roses!
Fainting! Flasks of Air!
Even for Death - a Fairy Medicine -
But, which is it - Sir?

(272)

The currant bushes that Emily's family grew were prolific. An entry in Vinnie's diary one July tells us that she got a farmer's early start that day. "Picked currants at four in morning. Made wine . . . " [50] Emily evidently assisted, as she bragged to Austin the following week that the wine would suit him.

Currant liquor sounds old-fashioned, but if you have a well-stocked bar you may be using it unawares. When you add crème de cassis to flavor mixed drinks, you

Raspberries "for the parching"

are using a syrup made from black currants. It is stronger and sweeter than the Dickinsons' currant wine, but definitely in the same family.

Wine was also an ingredient in another Dickinson favorite, wine jelly. Emily was the designated chef for this precursor to Jell-O. Once it firmed up, she slipped it out of its mold, flipping it upside down to display the raised pattern of a wheat sheaf or a rose. To a friend she quipped, "I shall make Wine Jelly Tonight and send you a Tumbler in the Letter, if the Letter consents, a Fabric sometimes obdurate." [51]

After supper is a perfect time for an evening constitutional in the garden. A pregnant moon emerges from the dusk, and the flower colors become like phosphorus. White flowers glow. Moths fly at night, resting with open wings on fragrant flowers like four-o'clocks. Fireflies blink, candles in the window of a summer night. Bats swoop.

⊰ MAKING WINE ⊱

Wine was regularly served in the Dickinson dining room. Currant wine was sweet and economical. Emily and Vinnie would have found this recipe in their mother's cookbook:

Those who have more currants than they have money, will do well to use no wine but of their own manufacture. Break and squeeze the currants, put three pounds and a half of sugar to two quarts of juice and two quarts of water. Put in a keg or barrel. Do not close the bung tight for three or four days, that the air may escape while it is fermenting. After it is done fermenting, close it up tight. Where raspberries are plenty, it is a great improvement to use half raspberry juice, and half currant juice. Brandy is unnecessary when the above-mentioned proportions are observed. It should not be used under a year or two. Age improves it. [52]

As summer progresses, so does the nocturnal decibel level in the garden, the crickets and cicadas joining in percussion and ostinato. But it is strangely soothing. Emily would be lulled to sleep by insect sounds:

Further in Summer than the Birds -
Pathetic from the Grass
A minor Nation celebrates
Its unobtrusive Mass.

No Ordinance be seen
So gradual the Grace
A pensive Custom it becomes
Enlarging Loneliness.

Antiquest felt at Noon
When August burning low
Arise this spectral Canticle
Repose to typify

Remit as yet no Grace
No Furrow on the Glow
Yet a Druidic Difference
Enhances Nature now

(895D)

And the season, which seemed unending, finally starts to shift. "*Summer?* My memory flutters - had I - was there a summer?" Emily wrote. "You should have seen the fields go - gay entomology! Swift little ornithology! Dancer, and floor, and cadence quite gathered away, and I, a phantom . . . rehearse the story! An orator of feather unto an audience of fuzz, - and pantomimic plaudits. 'Quite as good as a play,' indeed!" [53] With the applause of the insects, the season starts taking its bows.

Summer begins to have the look
Peruser of enchanting Book
Reluctantly but sure perceives
A gain upon the backward leaves.

Autumn begins to be inferred
By millinery of the cloud
Or deeper color in the shawl
That wraps the everlasting hill

The eye begins its avarice
A meditation chastens speech
Some Dyer of a distant tree
Resumes his gaudy industry

Conclusion is the course of all
Almost to be perennial
And then elude stability
Recalls to immortality -

(1693A)

Finally one morning in September, the air turns crisp, like cotton sheets hanging on the clothesline. Just breathing in makes Emily know that autumn has arrived.

The "minor Nation"
of late summer

A Late Summer Garden Primer

Butterflies will visit any garden, but if you include certain plants, they will drop by more often.

How to Create a Butterfly Utopia

Of butterflies and buttercups, Emily once wrote:

↶

The Butterfly's Assumption Gown
In Chrysoprase Apartments hung
This Afternoon put on -

How condescending to descend
And be of Buttercups the friend
In a New England Town -

(1329B)

To be a butterfly magnet, your garden needs to offer something at every stage, butterfly-wise. Choosy creatures, butterflies seek out particular host plants for their eggs and caterpillars. Some hospitable hosts are typical denizens of the flower and herb garden; others you might only see in a meadow. They include:

- Hollyhock (*Alcea rosea*)
- Dill (*Anethum graveolens*)
- Red clover (*Trifolium pratense*)
- Parsley (*Petroselinum crispum*)
- Common milkweed (*Asclepias syriaca*)
- New York ironweed (*Vernonia noveboracensis*)

Once the caterpillars withdraw into their chrysalis and emerge as butterflies, their needs change a bit. They need sun, a water source, and plenty of chow. Butterflies will seek out, after their meandering fashion, flowers with strong color and heavy fragrance in the same way we select dishes at a buffet by their presentation and smell. Because a butterfly needs to make a landing in order to eat, they will also choose flowers by their shape: composites, like daisies, panicles, like foxglove, and umbels, like Queen Anne's lace, all work well. A few flowers you might put on your butterfly shopping list are:

- Bee balm (*Monarda didyma*)
- Black-eyed Susan (*Rudbeckia hirta*)
- Butterfly weed (*Asclepias tuberosa*)
- Butterfly bush (*Buddleia davidii*)
- Common cosmos (*Cosmos bipinnatus*)
- Lantana (*Lantana camara*)
- Purple coneflower (*Echinacea purpurea*)
- Zinnia (*Zinnia elegans*)

So plant a butterfly garden, sit back and enjoy the new guests that condescend to visit in summer.

AUTUMN

A Gardener's Town

Autumn in New England has earned its reputation. Out Emily's window she sees the trees on the Pelham Hills turn into a warm palette. In her garden, small cyclones stir up leaves, rustling like pages in a book. Humidity evaporates, uncovering blue skies. There is a certain smell in the air: dry leaves, wood smoke, and an undertone of crispness.

The season is fair-haired; maples turn gold on the Dickinson grounds. In two early letters, Emily quotes Shakespeare's "sere and yellow leaf" to describe the color change.[1] The season is a siren.

The name - of it - is "Autumn" -
The hue - of it - is Blood -
An Artery - opon the Hill -
A Vein - along the Road -

Great Globules - in the Alleys -
And Oh, the Shower of Stain -
When Winds - upset the Basin -
And spill the Scarlet Rain -

It sprinkles Bonnets - far below -
It gathers ruddy Pools -
Then - eddies like a Rose - away -
Opon Vermillion Wheels -

(465)

"Spill the Scarlet Rain"

Like leaves in autumn, in the 1860s Emily must have suddenly felt old. Her eyes began to fail. Recent biographers Polly Longsworth and Alfred Habegger conclude that it was a condition called iritis, adhesions of the iris and lens that cause pain and extreme sensitivity to light. To be blind. Can a poet comprehend it? A gardener? It was intense enough to rouse her from her habit of seclusion.

⇥ HOW THE LEAVES TURN COLOR ⇤

Emily tells us in her poetic way that in the fall, the leaves grow old, the shorter days and cooler nights making them feel their age. The chlorophyll that makes them green starts to dissipate. The latent yellows and oranges show through, the chemistry of bananas and carrots. Leafy sugars are triggered to spin new colors, like red. The brightest displays come from dry weather; they're prolonged if the frost holds off. Eventually the leaves abdicate, the cellular glue weakening the connections between stem and plant, allowing them to drift away from the branches of the tree.

She left for Cambridge on her own for two protracted stays in a boardinghouse with Fanny and Loo, going for regular treatments for months. She was a refugee, missing home but making steady progress. To Sue, she sighed, "It would be best to see you - it would be good to see the Grass, and hear the Wind blow the wide way in the Orchard - Are the Apples ripe - Have the Wild Geese crossed - Did you save the seed to the pond Lily?"[2] It was as if she were a continent away.

When she came home finally to Amherst, she wrote her cousins, "For the first few weeks I did nothing but comfort my plants, till now their small green cheeks are covered with smiles."[3] Today we would call it horticultural therapy, the care lavished on plants creating its own brand of healing. For Emily it was simply inexpressible relief.

Scenes from a Town

The Amherst she returned to was a vibrant place. Thanks to Emily's father, the Amherst and Belchertown railroad had come to town in the 1850s, crossing Main Street not far to the east of the Homestead to pull into the new station. From the garden Emily could hear the whistle of the steam locomotive, the rumble of wheels on track. Across the Dickinson meadow, she could see the train veer off behind the hills, progress hidden by permanence.

Since her grandfather's time, Amherst had balanced between town and gown, and so did the Dickinsons. Edward Dickinson, longtime treasurer of the College, upheld a tradition of Commencement Day teas—an annual Wednesday open house for Amherst seniors, their professors, and local gentry. One can imagine them spilling out into the garden, discussing religion, politics, and war news. Mattie said that even the peonies were called "Commencement peonies." Emily continued to help her family host these teas, serving wine and conversation, well after she stopped going out into society.

If town was expanding, gown was also putting on new growth. The College continued its building program, adding, expanding, and updat-

The train approaches Amherst station south of the Dickinson Meadow.

ing its quarters. Additionally, during this time a new college came to town. The Morrill Land Grant Act, passed by Congress in 1862, reserved land in each state for an agricultural school. Massachusetts chose Amherst the following year. The first class was in session by 1867 at the Massachusetts Agricultural College, located north and west of the town center.

It was the site of an ornate palm house, the Durfee Plant House, a maharajah's tent in glass complete with fernery and fish pond. The glass house and President Clark's house, with its elegant landscaping and superb view, became a pleasant destination for an afternoon drive. Finished thirteen years after Mr. Dickinson built his daughter's, Mattie described the Plant House as "Aunt Emily's conservatory multiplied ever so many times." [4]

The proprietors of the Plant House bestowed cut flowers on their visitors—camellias, stephanotis, calla lilies—and sometimes immense quantities could be had for a small fee. Sue, a great flower arranger, availed herself of their largesse for her many fetes.

At Austin's request, Frederick Law Olmsted advised on improvements around the town proper. Olmsted also sketched a wide semicircle of trees for the village common. While his design was never specifically implemented, Austin and his cohorts planted many trees.

Austin liked to plant trees around the town partly for the fun of it and also for the good of the town. Austin's tree planting followed a town tradition—as early as 1840, engravings of the town center show regularly spaced street trees planted in front of the business establishments, protected from munching horses by wooden guards.

Think of Austin, usually tied down to his law practice, playing hooky on an overcast spring day. He would drive out in his carriage with hired men following in a wagon, armed with picks and shovels. Sometimes the children would come along. They would survey the areas

Tree planting in downtown Amherst in the 1840s

he knew in the surrounding hills, digging up saplings and small shrubs: mountain laurels, white pines, and small oaks, to name a few. In swampy areas they would find white dogwood and pink azalea. Back to town they would come, bringing their loot. All the plants were native to the area, which meant that they were, by definition, hardy and likely to thrive. Mattie remembered, "I loved the part in *Macbeth* where 'Birnam wood do come to Dunsinane.' Hadn't I seen Pelman woods come to Amherst many a time?"[5]

Tree Planting 101

As Austin knew, a tree is a marvelous thing. Its utility in shade, sap, nuts, and atmospheric exchange is unsurpassed. These days, we more often drive to the nursery and buy trees with credit cards rather than digging up woodland saplings. It's tidier, easier, and unquestionably legal. But domestic or wild, your tree planting will succeed if you follow a few simple steps in transplanting:

1. **Timing is everything.** If you want to plant a tree, try to do it in spring or fall, but not in the summer. It is hard enough for a tree to sustain the shock of adjusting to a new environment and set out new roots. The heat of the summer makes it almost impossible, evaporating moisture from the leaves and stressing the root system. In any season, be sure that the tree stays well watered until it is settled into its new home. If it dries out, the shock may kill it now, or even worse, kill it later when you've gone to all the trouble of tending it. In the off-season, Austin tagged the trees in the woods so that they would be easy to find, but didn't disturb them. You should do the same in the nursery.

2. **Out of the depths.** The most frequent mistake in planting a tree is burying it too deep. The flare of the trunk, where it widens at the base and forms its big main roots, should be exposed. If you look at a mature tree and the flare at its base, you'll get the idea. You'd think that nursery trees would come to you at the proper depth; not so. You will often have

to excavate from the top your potted or balled tree to find the flare. It may mean carefully carving away inches of soil and little adventitious roots. When you've found the flare, you will know how deep to dig.

3. **How to dig a hole.** Measure the size of the tree's container or root ball and dig a hole that will give it about six inches of clearance all the way around. Try to make it the same depth as the current soil of the pot or root ball.

4. **From the ground up.** Put the soil on a tarp and have a look at it. Remove any large rocks and crumble some soil between your fingers. Sometimes soil is depleted for one reason or another. On new building sites, contractors sometimes remove the topsoil, leaving a layer of dense substrata. If you've tried to dig through it with a shovel and find you need a pickaxe, you'll appreciate why it's called *hardpan.* "Concrete" would be more descriptive. In cases like these, you should dig as large a hole as you can stand and amend the soil with some organic matter: well-rotted manure, compost, or peat moss. Mix about one part compost to three parts soil, ending up with about 25 percent more volume than you started with.

5. **Neither girdles.** If you are planting a tree from a pot, be sure you open up the root ball. Inside a container, roots grow around and around, mimicking the shape of the pot. If you don't spread out the roots, they'll continue to grow that way, eventually girdling the trunk and dying. To give the roots elbow room, scratch them with a weeding fork or slice them vertically every six inches, cutting an inch deep.

6. **Nor corsets.** A balled-and-burlapped or caged tree presents different problems. Because it is recently dug, you want to keep the root ball intact. Frequently these trees are larger, which means you'll need the rope or wire for handles to lift the tree into the hole. But once the tree is in place, remove as much of the wire cage, burlap, and plastic rope as possible without breaking up the root ball. Burlap made of natural fiber will decompose, but at minimum, roll it away from the trunk of the tree.

7. **Fill 'er up.** Put the tree in the hole and start adding soil, tamping it down as you go. The trick is to avoid forming air pockets around the roots. If there isn't good soil contact, the roots will desiccate and die. When the hole is half full, water well, then finish adding soil up to the flare of the trunk. Water again. Current wisdom is to leave the newly planted tree unstaked, resulting in a stronger trunk and root mass over time.

8. **To mulch or not to mulch.** Mulching the soil around the base of a new plant helps to retain moisture and prevent weeds. Mulch no more than two inches deep and keep it away from the base of the plant. There's nothing worse than a mulch volcano, corroding the bark of a tree.

9. **Keep watering.** Trees need an inch of water a week during their first growing season—from April through November in northern climates. Until the ground freezes, keep on watering. Don't neglect them their second year either. By the third, they should be able to make it on their own, unless there is a severe drought.

Austin accomplished his tree planting in a most Victorian way, by forming a Village Improvement Society. On October 5, 1857, Austin and a group of like-minded gentlemen from the town got together with a purpose and formed the Amherst Ornamental Tree Association. With his legal training, Austin was well suited to serve on the executive committee and to draft the association's mission: "the laying out and ornamenting of the public common, the general improvement and adornment of the various public walks throughout the village by grading, graveling and lining with trees where there are deficiencies, and to do anything which may render the public grounds and ways of our village more attractive and beautiful." [6]

In his later years, Austin's landscape gardening efforts were even more ambitious. He laid out the Wildwood Cemetery outside of town, creating a miniature version of Mount Auburn. Wildwood's winding roads and rolling terrain gave him another venue for practicing the art of landscape gardening. Like Mount Auburn, the graves are tucked into their bucolic setting. Decades later, he was buried there.

It seems a shame that Emily didn't get out to watch many of Austin's efforts, but he made sure that she shared in some of them. One evening he enticed her to the edge of the Evergreens property to see the work he had done landscaping the new Congregational church across the street. Austin actually got into some hot water with his first gambit into ecclesiastical landscape design. One of the more conservative fellow parishioners almost quit the parish over the curved approach to the church door. "Not to walk straight up to the Throne of Grace was silly and heathenish—if it was not Papish—or worse."[7] But Austin won out in the end.

It's obvious from period photographs that some of Austin's street trees were planted in front of the Homestead. Then, as now, it pays to be related to someone on the Tree Association.

The Epitaph for an Elm

One of the street trees that Austin and the Village Improvement Society planted was the American elm, *Ulmus americana*. It grew in the local woods. Native to central New England, especially in areas of rich soil like the Connecticut River Valley, this tree was ideal for street use because of its distinctive shape. Its branches grow up and out from the crown, arching like a tall vase, made-to-order for shade above and visibility below. Its outline is one of a kind, a silhouette as special as Mona Lisa's smile. Once you've seen it, you can identify it at fifty-five miles an hour. However, only a few old examples remain in Amherst, lingering survivors of the Dutch elm disease epidemic.

Hope remains for a restoration of the elm, with propagation of a disease-resistant strain called the Liberty elm. The Elm Research Institute in Harrisville, New Hampshire, estimates that over a million of these new trees have been planted in the eastern United States over the past ten years.

Emily wouldn't have known Dutch elm disease specifically, but she knew some tree pathogens in order to be able to compose this poem:

Death is like the insect
Menacing the tree,
Competent to kill it,
But decoyed may be.

Bait it with the balsam,
Seek it with the saw,
Baffle, if it cost you
Everything you are.

Then, if it have burrowed
Out of reach of skill -
Wring the tree and leave it.
Tis the vermin's will.

(1783)

Some of the enterprising citizens of Amherst decided that a water cure could draw tourists to the town. Long a destination for locals—including Emily, who collected arbutus there—the springs in Pelham Hill two miles to the east of town became the site for a new hotel in 1860. Today, they would have bottled it, another Poland Spring or Perrier, but then they used it as an excuse to celebrate.

A year later, on July 6, 1861, the Springfield Republican reported on the anniversary of the health resort. There were patriotic songs, a brass band, poems, and of course, oration. "Speeches were made at the crowded dinner tables by Dr. Stearns, Dr. Hitchcock, and other officers of the college, Edward Dickinson and other gentlemen. . . . Dr. Hitchcock during his remarks gave the name of 'Hygean' to the mountain and springs, and christened the hotel the 'Orient.'" [8] Emily wasn't the only Amherst citizen given to the use of exotic names.

Emily was familiar with the efficacious properties attributed to the water, familiar with and facetious about them. One autumn she wrote of her sweet sultans, *Centaurea moschata*, "Aunt Katie and the Sultans have left the Garden now, and parting with my own, recalls their sweet companionship - Mine were not I think as exuberant as in other years - Perhaps the Pelham Water shocked their stately tastes." [9] While I somehow doubt that Emily actually brought Pelham to her plants, she had no hesitation in commenting on the types of people that would come to take the waters.

To the Show

An annual event that brought people to town was the Cattle Show. It was hosted by the East Hampshire Agricultural Society, founded May 1, 1850, by none other than Edward Dickinson, with his neighbor Luke Sweetser and other like-minded gentleman farmers. They intended the Society "for the encouragement of Agriculture and Mechanic Arts by Premiums and other means in the town of Amherst," [10] and their major event each year was the Cattle Show. Austin, in Boston at the time, wrote Susan's sister, "You don't know, Mat, how much I am anticipating in my visit. . . . I shall get my first and only view of autumn scenery for this year, then, and I think too, that Cattle Show day is the pleasantest in the whole year for Amherst. It seems a holiday especially for *Amherst people*, and not a lot of old women and ministers and students and the relatives and stuck-up trustees, as Commencement is." [11] Austin was right, if a bit rude.

An early morning artillery blast opened the event. Farmers came into town like agricultural Noahs, leading cows, pigs and sheep, horses and bulls, bleating and whinnying, lowing and stamping. The ladies of town vied against each other with baked goods, preserves, and fancy work, and in later years as culture inflicted itself on the town, fine arts and flower arrangements. Locals took sides on tractor pulls, probably with some money surreptitiously changing hands in the form of wagers.

Emily wrote:

〜

The Show is not the Show
But they that go -
Menagerie to me
My Neighbor be -
Fair Play -
Both went to see -

(1270B)

"Cattle Show day is the pleasantest in the whole year for Amherst"

Like any good county fair, the spirit of competition ruled, and the Dickinsons enthusiastically participated. In 1858, for example, Mrs. Dickinson was a flower judge, Austin chaired the fine arts category, and Mr. Dickinson judged the carriage horses. They also entered the competitions: Mrs. Dickinson bringing in her figs, Emily her bread, Sue her flowers. The local papers reported that Sue won fifty cents for her entry: "[A] basket and a vase of flowers were at once recognized by some of the Committee, as from the splendid garden of Mrs. W. A. Dickinson, whose diligence and success in the cultivation of flowers is only equaled by her surpassing skill in arranging them." [12] Even when Emily chose not to go herself, her family didn't forget her. "Austin and Sue have just returned from the Belchertown Cattle Show - Austin bought me a Balloon and Vinnie a Watermelon." [13]

Autumn in Emily Dickinson's Garden

"We go to sleep with the Peach in our Hands and wake with the Stone, but the Stone is the pledge of Summers to come." [14]

As Emily walks down the flagstone path into her garden, she notes, "We are by September and yet my flowers are bold as June." [15] A strange thing happens when the weather cools off in September. The garden, given a reprieve from the heat, comes out of its August doldrums to have a second flush of bloom. "There is not yet Frost, and Vinnie's Garden from the door looks like a Pond, with Sunset on it. Bathing in that heals her. How simple is Bethesda!" [16]

Summer has two Beginnings -
Beginning once in June -
Beginning in October
Affectingly again -

Without, perhaps, the Riot
But graphicker for Grace -
As finer is a going
Than a remaining Face -
Departing then - forever -
Forever - until May -
Forever is deciduous -
Except to those who die -

(1457)

The rose bushes open a few buds, as if putting a toe in the seasonal water. Emily once wrote a friend that their housekeeper, Maggie, "'dragged' the garden for this bud for you. You have heard of the 'last rose of summer.' This is that rose's son." [17] Their annual denial is tender, poignant.

Fall-blooming perennials like chrysanthemums, late daisies, and asters open in the flower beds. One September, Emily wrote to Sue, who was away on a visit, "Evenings get longer with the Autumn - that is nothing new! The Asters are pretty well. 'How are other blossoms?' 'Pretty well, I thank you.'" [18]

A Little Catalogue of Emily's Autumn Flowers

The flowers of autumn have a curious pungency, as if to emphasize the bittersweet end of the growing season with their sharp aroma. Their colors—purple, mauve, and gold—complement the trees as the green recedes from the canopy.

CHRYSANTHEMUM (*Dendranthema spp.*) Emily's old-fashioned mums were more modest than the bushy, overstimulated blobs of color called chrysanthemums today. Hers were like daisies rather than pompoms. Mattie said that they smelled like Thanksgiving. They came back faithfully from year to year. My personal favorites for old-fashioned mums are "Sheffield Pink" and "Clara Curtis." They bloom as single flowers in shades of pink.

ASTER (*Aster novae-angliae*) The aster is a star of autumn gardens: from the same root, etymologically speaking, as the ill-starred "disaster" and more recently, the star-sailing "astronaut." Its corona of pink, blue, or purple petals surrounding bright yellow and orange centers lights up the Dickinson meadow and fields across the northeast. So it's hardly surprising that it was dubbed the New England aster.

──────────────── ⇥| **TIP** |⇤ ────────────────

Both asters and mums like to be pinched—cut back in early June to half their size, then again in early July. It makes them branch and bloom more profusely. I suppose it is a handy response so that, if eaten by some grazing beast, the plant will seed more profusely. But for a gardener it is a bonus. Look for cultivars like the dwarf "Purple Dome" and bright pink "Alma Potschke."

MARIGOLDS (*Tagetes spp.*) Mattie used the name "merry gold," more comfortable to a descendent of Puritans than the original tribute to the Virgin Mary. Big, globe-shaped marigolds are called African marigolds (*Tagetes erecta*). Other more petite varieties are known as French (*Tagetes patula*). All of them are round-trip immigrants. Native to South and Central America, they went to the Old World with the European conquerors and came back with colonists.

"Merry gold"

⊰ **TIP** ⊱

Marigolds are annuals, but they are easy to grow from seed. They germinate easily indoors and transplant without fuss. Start with good drainage and full sun, and they require little care once they settle into the garden.

ARTEMESIA (*Artemesia spp.*) Mattie called artemesia "boy's love." Some of you may know it as southernwood or wormwood. But whatever you call it, artemesia looks more like an old man than a boy, its silvery grey foliage offsetting its green neighbors and the colors of flowers. Some varieties of artemesia are bullies, elbowing out gentler plants and showing up all over the garden with the tenacity of a weed. Others are better behaved. But most of them are easy to get from a neighbor or a gardening friend. A small division of root and stem will get it going in your border.

Artemesia is always grey, but in Emily's autumn garden the foliage on other perennials start to turn, adding color to the canvas. Peonies' lobed leaves turn a purple red.

-⇥ WHEN IS DIVISION LIKE MULTIPLICATION? ⇤-

Division is a way to make more perennials, dividing up a clump to make more plants. The rule of thumb for perennials is to divide spring-blooming flowers in the fall, fall-blooming flowers in the spring. But actually most perennials will stand division in either spring or fall, if you don't mind sacrificing some of the bloom. Cool weather is best—less stressful for both plant and gardener. If you look at mature clumps, you might see the center of the plant looking less vigorous than the outside: fewer leaves and bloom stalks. That indicates a time to split.

Division takes a certain fearlessness. I generally dig out the whole plant and spade or fork it apart. An easy way to divide fibrous rooted plants like Siberian iris is to insert two garden forks back-to-back in the clump, then lever the forks against each other. Presto, the clump splits apart.

The old parts of the plant get added to the compost bin. The new growth is split up to become your stock of new plants. Decide where you want them in the border, and replant them with some fresh compost added to the soil in the planting holes. By dividing and replanting in September or early October, you give the plants sufficient time to settle in and set some roots before the ground freezes.

If there's no room in the garden and you can't bear to compost the extras, you have a few choices: Give them to friends. Find a garden club that is sponsoring a plant sale. Or sponsor a plant swap where everyone brings a plant and takes one home.

———⊰❙ **HOW TO PAMPER YOUR PEONIES** ❙⊱———

Autumn is the season to plant or transplant peonies in order to take advantage of the peony's dormant period over the winter. The peony prospers in a planting hole that is deep and extremely well amended. Dig a hole that is three feet wide and two feet deep in a sunny location, and put in extra shovels of compost. Peonies are long-lived, so the extra work is worth it. The secret is in the planting depth. If they are too deep, they won't flower well.

If you look at a peony's thick, fleshy roots you will see one or more little buds or "eyes." Plant these just below the surface of the soil. Water well with a mild fish emulsion fertilizer, and mulch lightly to avoid burying the eyes.

Cool-Weather Vegetables

The Dickinson vegetable garden was planted with winter in mind, boasting thick-skinned squash that would hold until the spring. Emily joked with one correspondent, "Gentlemen here have a way of plucking the tops of trees, and putting the fields in their cellars annually, which in point of taste is execrable, and would they please omit, I should have fine vegetation & foliage all the year round, and never a winter month."[19]

Winter squash grow on great sprawling vines. Mattie remembered that the vines "trailed over everything the summer left behind right up to frost."[20] In order to keep properly, the squash have to stay on their vigorous vines until they are fully mature. The rinds are tough and inedible, but the inner fruit stays firm.

Some of the squash were no doubt Hubbards, the most popular variety in America after their introduction in the 1840s. The huge,

Chinese shoe–shaped fruits originated from a single squash. A sea captain brought one to a woman in Marblehead, Massachusetts: vegetative bounty from a voyage to the West Indies or to South America. The woman planted seeds from the squash, and later shared her success by passing seeds on to a Mrs. Elizabeth Hubbard. She in turn gave them to a seedsman, and acquired the fame of association with a wonderful and quirky curcubit (member of the squash family) when he introduced the seeds onto the market.

Mattie also tells us of purple and green cabbages and of rows of celery banked for winter. Cabbages and celery both appreciate cooler weather. The cabbages form great globes surrounded by haloes of looser leaves. Thanks to Mattie, we know that they grew at least two varieties, adding to the color of the dishes served in the Dickinson dining room.[21]

Celery is planted in trenches like rows of toy soldiers, six to eight inches apart, making them easier to manage. The plants are banked up with soil as they grow, blanching the outer stalks for sweetness and tenderness. By autumn only the top leaves show. Nowadays, blanching plants like celery and asparagus isn't as popular because green vegetables have more nutrients. Along with bitterness, vitamins disappear. But the Dickinsons and their neighbors were more concerned with flavor. Banking celery also lets you put them in the bank well past frost, since the soil effectively makes a mini–root cellar for each plant.

When the frosts come, root vegetables are gathered into the cellar.

The Products of my Farm are these
Sufficient for my Own
And here and there a Benefit
Unto a Neighbor's Bin.

Great spheres of cabbage grew in the Dickinsons' vegetable garden.

With us, 'tis Harvest all the Year
For when the Frosts begin
We just reverse the Zodiac
And fetch the Acres in -

(1036)

It is harvest time in Amherst, a time for sharing bounty.

A Season of Nut and Fruit

In autumn, nuts bounce onto the ground, animating the season in an orgy of seed dispersal before the winter dormancy.

Acorns from the Homestead's white oak thump down. Squirrels harvest them, making a subject for a poem if you are a poet of a particular breed.

A Saucer holds a Cup
In sordid human Life
But in a Squirrel's estimate
A Saucer holds a Loaf -

A Table of a Tree
Demands the little King
And every Breeze that run along
His Dining Room do swing -

His Cutlery - he keeps
Within his Russet Lips -
To see it flashing when he dines
Do Birmingham eclipse -

Acorn

Convicted - could we be
Of our Minutiae
The smallest Citizen that flies
Is heartier than we -

(1407)

Black walnuts fall sheathed in their thick green skins. They need to be carefully dried and peeled before cracking, or your fingers will be dyed green for days. Hickories are buttery, but are literally a tough nut, needing a heavy hand and a heavier hammer. The chestnuts are ripe, splitting their burrs. Emily went chestnutting when she was young, a family outing or an excursion with friends to the trees that grew on the Flat Hills. Roasting them on the stove or in a fireplace, their succulent flesh was a taste specific unto the season.

Chestnuts were more than metaphoric. To describe herself, Emily once said, "I am small, like the Wren, and my Hair is bold, like the Chestnut Bur - and my eyes, like the Sherry in the Glass, that the Guest leaves." [22] Emily also used chestnuts to indicate time. "I havn't felt quite as well as usual since the Chestnuts were ripe," she told her Aunt Libbie, "though it wasn't the Chestnuts' fault." [23]

Looking forward to a visit from a friend, Samuel Bowles, she described his schedule this way. "We reckon your coming by the Fruit. When the Grape gets by - and the Pippin, and the Chestnut - when the Days are a little short by the clock - and a little long by the want - when the sky has new Red Gowns - and a Purple Bonnet." [24] Unfortunately, like the elm, the American chestnut proved susceptible to an imported pest and no longer graces Amherst byways. Emily could easily reckon time by the grapes, since their trellises stood in front of the barn, shielding the barnyard from view, and getting the good air circulation that grapevines desire.

It's likely that some of the grapes on the Homestead's trellises were Concords, Massachusetts born and bred. On his Concord farm, a gentleman named Ephraim Wales Bull culled through more than twenty thousand seedlings of American grapes until he hit upon the Concord in 1849. It ripened early with a rich flavor. Four years later, Mr. Bull felt ready for prime time. He arranged the first bunches of his Concord grapes to display before the public at the Horticultural Exhibition in Boston, and came away with the blue ribbon.

In the autumn, the grapes hang down from their trellises blue, white, and purple, a fable of Aesop ripening in the full sun. One October, Emily described the monarchy to Austin: "The grapes too are fine, juicy, and such a purple - I fancy the robes of kings are not a tint more royal. The vine looks like a kingdom, with ripe round grapes for subjects - the first instance on record of subjects devouring kings!" [25]

Mrs. Dickinson's three fig trees grow on the opposite side of the grape arbor, sheltered from the winter winds and getting reflected heat off the barn. Their leaves are arabesques, Moorish architecture at home in the Alhambra. And the trees were prolific. Even the journalist in the local gazette reported receiving her fresh figs. Nothing like a fresh fruit press release.

Giving a Fig About Figs

To me, "fig" was always directly connected to "Newton," the soft, chewy cookie in a bright yellow box. As I got old enough to do the grocery shopping, my fig world expanded to brown shriveled things packed with their buddies in a plastic box in the produce section, labeled "Product of California." I was past thirty when I tasted my first garden fig. It was a revelation, a broad-hipped, succulent delight in the shape of an inverted balloon. Small wonder that journalist waxed poetic about Mrs. Dickinson's offerings. He said, "We have received from Mrs. Edward Dickinson, a plate of delicious ripe figs. The great rarity of this fruit, in this latitude, renders the gift peculiarly acceptable at this time." [26]

Fig trees (*Ficus carica*) are Mediterranean natives, more suited to the Costa del Sol than the Pioneer Valley of Massachusetts. But with patience and persistence, you can gather northern figs.

• **Select.** There are lots of varieties of figs, and you can still buy the ones that were available in the Dickinsons' day. (See the Resources.) A New Englander would call my favorite "Brown Turkey"; the French call it "Aubique Noire." Slice into its dark skin and you'll find a reddish pulp the color of a good Merlot. It is particularly cold-hardy. Another is "White Marseilles," the Italian honey fig, super-sweet with yellow-green skin and pale flesh.

• **Plant.** Position your sun-worshipping figs in the hottest spot you have in the garden. Figs want to extend a deep taproot and grow into large trees. But if you want the maximum amount of fruit in a cold climate, it's best to contain their enthusiasm. You can grow them in a fourteen-inch pot, though it will require daily watering in the summer. The alternative, one probably used by Mrs. Dickinson, is to grow the fig in a deep trench that is lined with stones, tiles, or pot shards. It seems a bit counterintuitive, but if you restrict the tree's growth, it puts more effort into fruit production. Soil should be a bit lean—not overly fertile, that is. A fertilized fig will put all its energy into making leaves rather than fruit.

• **Prune.** Cut back your fig in late winter, but don't cut too far. Northern figs fruit on last year's wood; in fact, you should be able to see the small embryos developing alternately near joints along the branches. While it might seem odd, it's good horticultural practice to also remove in March any fruit embryos that are larger than a pea. The larger embryos don't mature, and they will draw strength from the viable fruit.

Figs, the great rarity of Emily's mother

• **Pick.** If you are in the north, trees will only bear one crop of figs per season. Don't be disappointed not to see flowers. The flowers are actually inside the developing fruit. If you don't plan to eat them as fresh figs, you can let the fruit dry on the tree; it drops of its own accord and in its own good time. If your figs start to attract unwanted birds, you can cover them with deer netting or a fishing net.

• **Protect.** In a climate like Amherst's, fig trees have to be wrapped, buried, or brought inside during winter. You can fit the trunks with foam rubber pipe insulation and wrap the branches in burlap stuffed with straw. If you grow the fig in a trench, you can bend the branches and bury them. Or you can bring a potted fig onto a heated porch. Emily's mother, and the Dickinsons' hired men, probably buried their trees.

If a garden is a reflection of the gardener, what do three fig trees tell of Mrs. Dickinson? She would take on a challenge, she savored the exotic, and she appreciated a deep root.

The Orchard

The orchard appears over and over again in Emily's poems. She even posits that we're "Orchard sprung."

The Robin's my Criterion for Tune -
Because I grow - where Robins do -
But, were I Cuckoo born -
I'd swear by him -
The ode familiar - rules the Noon -
The Buttercup's, my whim for Bloom -
Because, we're Orchard sprung -
But, were I Britain born,
I'd Daisies spurn -

None but the Nut - October fit -
Because - through dropping it,
The Seasons flit - I'm taught -
Without the Snow's Tableau
Winter, were lie - to me -
Because I see - New Englandly -
The Queen, discerns like me -
Provincially -

(256)

A Little Catalogue of Emily's Apples

In the Dickinsons' autumn orchard, apples ripen and fall in ongoing acts of gravity. It is a fine opportunity for Emily's commentary. "Men are picking up the apples to-day, and the pretty boarders are leaving the trees, birds and ants and bees. I have heard a chipper say "dee" six times in disapprobation. How should we like to have our privileges wheeled away in a barrel?"[27]

The apples from the Dickinson orchard were the source of another staple for the table: cider—both fresh and, of course, fermented. There was a local cider press where the Dickinsons brought their apples. "The cider is almost done - we shall have some I guess by Saturday, at *any rate by Sunday noon!*"[28]

GOLDEN SWEETING They are yellow apples, large and pale. In the Dickinson orchard, they were even sweeter because of the nostalgia. "The Aunt that has shared her Blossoms with me, must have a cluster of mine." Emily wrote, "The Golden Sweets are from Grandfather's Tree."[29]

RUSSET The russets are rough, their surfaces reminding someone of the homespun cloth that is their namesake. Mr. Dickinson would have called them "good keepers." Put in the cellar in November, they will keep until June. In point of fact they're not the most tasty apples, but if you wanted an apple pie in the spring in nineteenth-century Amherst, russets were a good bet.

◠

It is an honorable Thought
And makes One lift One's Hat
As One met sudden Gentlefolk
Opon a daily Street

That We've immortal Place
Though Pyramids decay
And Kingdoms, like the Orchard
Flit Russetly away

(1115)

BALDWIN Bright red, crisp, and juicy, the Baldwins originated in Massachusetts from a chance seedling, much like a certain poet. They are prolific, unless there is an unexpected cold snap in spring. Emily complained to one correspondent, "We have no Fruit this year, the Frost having barreled that in the Bud - except the 'Fruits of the Spirit,' but Vinnie prefers Baldwins." [30] When she said "fruits of the spirit," she was quoting Galatians.

And More Fruit Trees

The orchard minded its p's and q's: peaches, pears, plums, and quinces, and Emily mingled their juices in her letters. To one friend, she was effervescent: "It was so delicious to see you - a Peach before the time, it makes all seasons possible and Zones—a caprice." [31] To another, she penned an admonition against joint correspondence to her and Vinnie: "A mutual plum is not a plum. I was too respectful to take the pulp and do not like the stone." [32] Plum and pear trees stood to the east of the Homestead. Her description of sugar pears is luscious: "Hips like hams, and the flesh of bonbons." [33]

The quince bushes were called japonicas, a nod to their origins. There was at least one on the Dickinson property. Mattie talks about sitting under the japonica. And the Dickinson women preserved quinces as well. Mrs. Jameson, one of their neighbors, told her son that "Vinnie sent me over some lovely quinces yesterday so I shall have something nice for the winter." [34]

Autumn is fruitful in another sense. It is a season to inspire poets, including Emily, who reported as the season faded that:

"Hips like hams, and the flesh of bonbons"

Besides the autumn poets sing
A few prosaic days
A little this side of the snow
And that side of the Haze.
A few incisive mornings -
A few ascetic eves -
Gone - Mr. Bryant's "Golden Rod"
And Mr. Thom'son's "Sheaves" -
Still, is the bustle in the brook,
Sealed, are the spicy valves.
Mesmeric fingers softly touch
The eyes of many Elves -

Perhaps a *squirrel* may remain,
My sentiments to share -
Grant me O Lord a sunny mind -
Thy windy will to bear!

    (123A)

⇥ POETS SING OF AUTUMN ⇤

Finding Emily's gardens has been an unraveling, following threads and gossamers. Who were Mr. Bryant and Mr. Thomson, anyway?

Bryant—William Cullen Bryant (1794–1878)—is interesting to compare to Emily. He was born and raised in Cummington, Massachusetts, less than twenty-five miles from Amherst. His claim to fame was as a poet and the longtime editor of the *New York Evening Post*. Among other things, he lobbied for the creation of a large park in Manhattan, which ultimately became Central Park. In 1864, he wrote a poem entitled *My Autumn Walk,* which includes the line, "The goldenrod is leaning, and the purple aster waves." [35] It is an ode to the season, and to the Civil War.

Mr. Thomson, on the other hand, was not from Massachusetts, not even from America. James Thomson (1700–1748) was a British poet whose epic poem *The Seasons* is considered a breakthrough. It was the first major work to have Nature front and center. English romantics like William Wordsworth took a cue from it. Haydn used a translation of the poem as a libretto for an oratorio. Evidently Thomson left his mark on Dickinson as well when writing, "Crown'd with the sickle and the wheaten sheaf, while Autumn, nodding o'er the yellow plain, comes jovial on." [36]

The weather can't make up its mind, and a late warm snap is a golden memory. The original inhabitants thought it a gift from a benevolent southern god, thus the name "Indian summer." That string of fine days lures the gardener into thinking that perhaps, just once, the year will run in reverse.

These are the days when Birds come back -
A very few - a Bird or two,
To take a final look -

These are the days when skies resume
The old - old sophistries of June -
A blue and gold mistake.

Oh fraud that cannot cheat the Bee.
Almost thy plausibility
Induces my belief,

Till ranks of seeds their witness bear,
And softly thro' the altered air
Hurries a timid leaf -

Oh sacrament of summer days!
Oh last Communion in the Haze -
Permit a Child to join -

Thy sacred emblems to partake -
Thy consecrated bread to take -
And thine immortal wine -

(122A)

An alert Emily watches for the right day to dig up plants from the border and carry the pots into the conservatory. It is a balancing act, as most plants benefit from the cool evenings. "The plants went into camp last night," she says in one letter; "[T]heir tender armor insufficient for the crafty nights." [37]

Outside-In

What we call houseplants are typically tropical. They bask on the piazza in the heat of August, but when the mercury dips toward freezing, they won't make it outside. Thus they are also termed *tender perennials*. In Florida, they would live outdoors year-round, but not in New England.

As Emily knew, in summering plants outdoors timing is everything. I learned this the hard way one year, when my huge, prolific African violet turned into lime mush in one frosty night. So every September the rabbit's foot and button ferns come in first, along with the spider plant. Great-Grandma Hegele's Christmas cactus stays out a week or two longer, since the shorter days and cooler nights signal it to set buds. Moved to a cool room without artificial lighting, the cactus blooms between Thanksgiving and New Year's, true to its name.

Here are a few tips for bringing in your potted plants:

• While we don't all have Emily's conservatory, find a sunny, cool window for your plants' winter vacation. If there is too much heat, leaves will desiccate, curling up from the edges and eventually dropping.

• Try to give your winter houseguests more humidity. Mist from a sprayer will do, or set the pots on a tray filled with pebbles and water.

• Check the plants for pests, which often lay eggs when the pots are outside. Spider mites leave tiny webs. Scale looks like small oval pods stuck to the underside of the leaves. White fly are tiny little white dots. Especially look on the stems and under the leaves. For an easy (and environmentally sound) pest control, dilute a small amount of Ivory soap in water, and spray it or wipe it on the leaves, top and bottom.

• Moving plants indoors "is one of the parting acts of the year and has an emerald pathos - ," Emily wrote, "and Austin hangs bouquets of corn in the piazza's ceiling, also an omen, for Austin believes."[38] As Emily knew and Austin believed, gardening is one part incantation.

In the Dickinson meadows the goldenrod is yellow; the asters are purple. Worker bees are frantically gathering pollen into the hives. In the hills around Amherst the gentians bloom, a shockingly blue flower, blue like the pigment straight from a tube of paint.

God made a little Gentian -
It tried - to be a Rose -
And failed - and all the Summer laughed -
But just before the Snows

There rose a Purple Creature -
That ravished all the Hill -
And Summer hid her Forehead -
And Mockery - was still -

The Frosts were her condition -
The Tyrian would not come
Until the North - invoke it -
Creator - Shall I - bloom?

(520)

In the woodlands, witch hazel lets down its yellow hair. Witch hazel is a large shrub, *Hamamelis virginiana*, inhabiting the edges of the forest around Amherst. Emily described it best. She called a witch hazel bloom "a lovely alien," [39] and it does have that sci-fi movie look. When Fanny and Loo sent her a sprig, Emily told them, "It looked like tinsel fringe combined with staider fringes, witch and witching too, to my joyful mind.... Is there not a dim suggestion of a dandelion, if her hair were raveled and she grew on a twig instead of a tube, - though this is timidly submitted." [40]

Finding the first bloom of a wild plant was something of a competitive sport in Amherst among Emily's set. One spring, after a friend brought her some arbutus, Emily said, "Yours was the first arbutus. It was a rosy boast." Then she threw down the gauntlet with: "I will send you the first witch hazel." [41]

Some plants come to the gardener, rather than the other way around. And autumn is the season for hitchhikers.

A Burdock twitched my Gown
Not Burdock's blame - but mine
Who went too near the Burdock's Den -

A Bog affronts my shoe.
What else have Bogs to do -
The only art they know
The splashing men?

'Tis Minnows - should despise -
An Elephant's calm eyes
Look further on.

(289B)

Amherst has a relatively short growing season. The first frost can hit before October, only five months from the last frost in May. Emily once wrote, "In early Autumn we had Mid-winter Frost - 'When God is with us, who shall be against us,' but when he is against us, other allies are useless." [42] The frost is a disturbing lover.

    🙋

A Visitor in Marl -
Who influences Flowers -
Till they are orderly as Busts -
And Elegant - as Glass -

Who visits in the Night -
And just before the Sun -
Concludes his glistening interview -
Caresses - and is gone -

But whom his fingers touched -
And where his feet have run -
And whatsoever Mouth he kissed -
Is as it had not been -

    (558)

In another letter she confesses that "Veils of Kamchatka dim the Rose, in my Puritan garden." [43] In a letter to one of her aunts, Emily once said, "I trust your Garden was willing to die - I do not think that mine was - it perished with beautiful reluctance, like an Evening Star." [44] Autumn's end is stark, the trees bare and the ground exposed. Emily dreams of leapfrogging the winter, and finding the spring that follows.

    🙋

We should not mind so small a flower -
Except it quiet bring
Our little garden that we lost
Back to the Lawn again -

So spicy her Carnations nod -
So drunken reel her Bees -
So silver, steal a hundred Flutes
From out a hundred trees -

That whoso sees this little flower,
By faith, may clear behold
The Bobolinks around the throne
And Dandelions gold.

(82A)

An Autumn Garden Primer

Autumn was the time that Emily and Vinnie cleaned up the garden, trimming and mulching the perennials, roses, and strawberries with borrowed straw from the barn's loft or composted manure from the barnyard.

Putting Your Garden to Bed

To avoid the deadly sin of sloth, it's time to get your own garden ready for winter. It's time:

• For taking cuttings and rescuing tender bulbs, if that's your nature. Emily certainly did. The dahlias can be dug just after the frost kills the foliage. Store the tubers in peat moss in a cool, dry place (thirty-five to forty-five degrees).

• For fall cleanup. Or at least, that's what the experts say. I tend to like the look of the garden after the frost and during the snow season. The silhouettes of round globe thistles and sedum flowers add interest to the winter garden. So, if you're so inclined, you can wait until one of those fine days in February or early March to do a pre-spring cleanup instead. If you do a fall cleanup, wait until the first hard frost to cut back stems and leaves from the perennials. As long as the leaves are green, they are still producing food for the plant.

• For protecting your marginally hardy plants, if, like Emily, you live north of the Mason-Dixon line. In Amherst, the roses were hilled up with compost. Remove as many dead leaves as possible from around the plants and make a mound of compost or mulch three inches deep around the base of each plant. If you garden in a climate with any humidity, you'll find that most of your roses drop some leaves in the summer. If they are yellowed and spotty, they have black spot, a fungal disease. By being scrupulous in your cleanup, you'll forego the spread of the disease next year.

• For taking inventory. Do the daisies need to be divided? Are you ready to root out the lilac that looks so scraggly, or can it be rejuvenated by a hard pruning? I also take some pictures around the garden, so that when the catalogues start rolling in, I can stare at the current denizens of the border and decide if I can squeeze in one more plant. A few notes and snapshots can help you muse about your garden, even in the bleak midwinter.

• For planting spring-flowering bulbs, at least until the ground freezes. To reap the benefits of those daffodil dowries, you need to invest time and effort now. If you plant them in the dozens, you may want to find some hired help.

WINTER

Requiem for a Gardener

Winter in Amherst is dark. Days abbreviate. On the first day of winter the sun sets around 4:30.

Winter brings memories of the sledding parties and sleigh rides of Emily's youth. In front of the Homestead, Main Street wasn't plowed. The snow was packed down; runners replaced wheels on the carriages and sleighs came out of stables. Sleighs were so quiet, they needed bells to warn pedestrians. Winter was made of "days of jingling bells," she wrote to her Uncle Joseph Sweetser. [1] Children skated on the shallow, frozen places across the street in the Dickinson meadow.

The weather is changeable. When Emily was young, she enthused, "Haven't we had delightful weather for a week or two? It seems as if Old Winter had forgotten himself. Don't you believe he is absent-minded?" [2] Later in life, Emily described the erratic weather with more mature prose: "It storms in Amherst five days - it snows, and then it rains, and then soft fogs like vails hang on all the houses, and then the days turn Topaz, like a lady's pin." [3] Clear skies are often draped with high, icy

Main Street, Amherst, circa 1900

cirrus clouds that look like the shadows cast by a Venetian blind. Before storms, clouds are thick and grey. It smells like snow.

The depth of the season can be measured in snowfall. For much of the winter, Emily's garden is snow-covered, a moonscape. The snow is a cold blanket that prevents the thawing and freezing that heaves plants out of the ground and kills tender roots.

When Emily's garden is exposed, it is full of ghosts. Perennials like peonies die to the ground, leaving carapaces of stems and dried leaves. Their watery stems solidify in the first freezes, then evaporate under the winter sun. Grey leaves and hollow stems, the last burst of inflorescence are now dried.

There's a certain Slant of light,
Winter Afternoons -
That oppresses, like the Heft
Of Cathedral Tunes -

Heavenly Hurt, it gives us -
We can find no scar,
But internal difference -
Where the Meanings, are -

None may teach it - Any -
'Tis the Seal Despair -
An imperial affliction
Sent us of the Air -

When it comes, the Landscape listens -
Shadows - hold their breath -
When it goes, 'tis like the Distance
On the look of Death -

(320)

The last years of Emily's life were a winter of loss. Her father died suddenly in 1874, leaving Emily, her mother, and her sister behind in the Homestead. The ways she missed her father were a litany: the bread she baked for him in particular, the gravitational pull he exerted from the moment he walked through the door, the plants he bought for her garden. That winter, she stared out her window at the stark landscape, conjuring his memory, fingering the pages of a wildflower book he inscribed to her many years before. She called it an "austere Afternoon," describing the gut-wrenching grief with her pen: "The Hand that plucked the Clover - I seek ... No event of Wind or Bird breaks the Spell of Steel. Nature squanders Rigor - now - where she squandered Love. Chastening - it may be - the Lass that she receiveth. My House is a House of Snow - true - sadly - of few." [4]

The following year, her mother suffered a debilitating stroke, leaving her an invalid and sealing her daughter's reclusiveness, with little to comfort Emily except the solace of the garden, even the winter garden bereft of flowers. "I do not go away, but the Grounds are ample - almost travel - to me - and the few that I knew - came - since my Father died." [5] Within the house, the two sisters cared for their mother for more than a decade until she died in 1882. Up and down the back stairs they went, bringing her special food or a blossom from the garden. Vinnie later wrote of their mother, "She was so fond of every bird & flower & so full of pity for every grief." [6]

Then, close on to her mother's death, came the hardest loss of all, next door at the Evergreens. Eight-year-old Gib, Thomas Gilbert, Emily's youngest nephew, died of typhoid in 1883. Her house *was* a house of snow.

She went from tending people to tending graves, the small cemetery just a short distance from the house. She and Vinnie walked up the hill and decorated the graves with flowers during the growing season: lily of the valley for Gib, flowering branches of hawthorn for their parents.

Emily felt submerged in death; how could she help thinking of her own? "When it shall come my turn," she mused in a letter, "I want

The Dickinson Homestead in winter, 1880s

a Buttercup - Doubtless the Grass will give me one, for does she not revere the whims of her flitting Children?"[7] All the regrets surfaced, the bittersweet hope of a next life. "I wish, until I tremble, to touch the ones I love before the hills are red - are gray - are white - are 'born again'! If we knew how deep the crocus lay, we never should let her go."[8]

Even with her bereavement, Emily continued to see a circle of close friends and, in her way, to make new ones. Her correspondence never ebbed, and in some cases increased.

"*You Are a Great Poet—*"

Helen Hunt Jackson (nee Fiske) was born in Amherst in 1830, the same year as Emily, and the two grew up together. Helen's mother, worrying that she was too much of a tomboy, wrote to her in 1841, "As to playing in the barn and shed I would rather have you play in the house; and in the garden when it is pleasant, you will make more washing if you are round in such places, the weather is becoming cold, too, and they are not so proper for Misses as within doors and in the garden."[9]

Helen and Emily were schoolmates for a time in primary school at Amherst, and they both had an interest in gardening. Helen corresponded with her parents about planting flower seeds and her garden with moss pinks, irises, roses, and honeysuckle. In June 1846, while she was studying at Ipswich Female Academy, her father wrote:

> If you study Botany, I hope you will keep an Herbarium, not putting into it every weed that grows, but collecting choice flowers, & writing out a scientific description of each—adding to it any extract—fine in sentiment or language that you may meet with or remember, or sometimes a passage composed by yourself, in which there is a happy allusion to the flower.[10]

Emily and Helen met again in 1860, after Helen had married Major Hunt. Emily was charmed with them both. Emily particularly

remembered the major saying that "her great dog 'understood gravi-
tation.'" [11] After Major Hunt died, Helen turned to writing as a pro-
fession: essays, fiction, children's books, a book on wildflowers, and
poems. Her poems include floral allusions such as this verse from
"Where?":

> My snowy eupatorium has dropped
> Its silver threads of petals in the night;
> No signal told its blossoming had stopped;
> Its seed-films flutter silent, ghostly white:
> No answer stirs the shining air,
> As I ask, "Where?" [12]

By chance, Helen was introduced to Thomas Wentworth Higgin-
son, who encouraged her efforts. Learning Helen was from Amherst, he
showed her some of the unusual poems he had received from Emily.
Helen was enchanted, and she became the lone voice to push Emily to
publish during her lifetime. "You are a great poet—" Helen wrote
prophetically, "and it is wrong to the day you live in, that you will not
sing aloud. When you are what men call dead, you will be sorry you
were so stingy." [13] Tantalizingly few of their letters survive; surely they
would have mentioned their flowers.

We know they were looking out into their gardens, watching
birds. In 1879, Emily sent Helen a poem about a bluebird. Impressed,
Helen replied, "We have blue birds here—I might have had the sense
to write something about one myself, but I never did: and now I never
can." [14] She lays down a challenge at the end of her letter: "What should
you think of trying your hand on the oriole? He will be along presently."
Emily responds magnificently with the poem, "One of the ones that
Midas touched," dubbing the oriole "a Pleader," "a Dissembler," "an Epi-
cure," "a Thief." [15] Not to be one-upped, she writes to Helen, "To the Ori-
ole you suggested I add a Humming Bird and hope they are not
untrue." [16] The hummingbird she adds is a tour de force.

〜

A Route of Evanescence
With a revolving Wheel
A Resonance of Emerald
A Rush of Cochineal
And every Blossom on the Bush
Adjusts its tumbled Head -
The Mail from Tunis, probably,
An easy Morning's Ride -

(1489B)

One of Helen's novels, *Mercy Philbrick's Choice*, published in 1876 was said by some to draw on Emily Dickinson's life. Scholars today say it is autobiographical. Yet it is a reflection of the life of an Amherst woman with horticultural and literary interests. Small wonder that there is overlap, since they grew up together.[17] It describes Mercy's garden which sounds like both of theirs, "the quaint, trim beds of old-fashioned pinks and ladies' delights and sweet williams which bordered the little path." [18] It describes her collecting woodland specimens:

There were three different species of ground-pine in these woods, and hepatica and pyrola and winter-green and thickets of laurel. What wealth for a lover of wild, out-door things! Each day Mercy bore home new treasures, until the house was almost as green and fragrant as a summer wood. [19]

And there is a description of a room bursting with plants:

A pressed cloverleaf from
the frontispiece of
Mercy Philbrick's Choice

There were evergreen trees in boxes; the window-seats were filled
with pots of green things growing; waving masses of ferns hung
down from brackets on the walls.[20]

After *Mercy Philbrick's Choice* was published, Helen convinced
Emily to allow her to submit the poem "Success is counted sweetest"
anonymously to the *No Name Series*, where it was published in 1878 in
an anthology called *The Masque of Poets*. She asked to be named literary
executor in Emily's will, but died first in 1885—another loss for Emily.

Amherst's New Belle

Mabel Loomis Todd was a new friend late in Emily's life. Mabel made
her grand entrance in September 1881 with her husband, David, the new
astronomy professor at Amherst College. She sang and played the piano,
wrote and painted. With her youth, good looks, and accomplishments,
she must have seemed phosphorescent to the Dickinson siblings. Susan
immediately recruited Mabel and David as dinner guests at the Ever-
greens. Mabel often visited next door, talking to Vinnie, singing, and
playing the parlor piano with Emily listening from the hallway or the
top of the stairs. After the Beethoven or Bach or Scarlatti, Emily would
send in a tray to the parlor with a poem, a glass of sherry, or a rose to
reward the performance. She would even talk to Mabel through a closed
door on occasion.

While Emily never met Mabel face-to-face, she did count her as a
friend who shared her interest in plants. Mabel wrote to her parents,
"Soon after I came home a box of the most exquisite flowers came for
me—hyacinths, heliotrope, and some odd yellow flowers which I do not
know—from—who do you imagine? Miss Emily Dickinson!"[21]

Mabel painted botanicals. In 1882, when in Washington, she sent
Emily a wooden panel painted with Indian pipes. Emily responded
ecstatically, "That without suspecting it you should send me the pre-

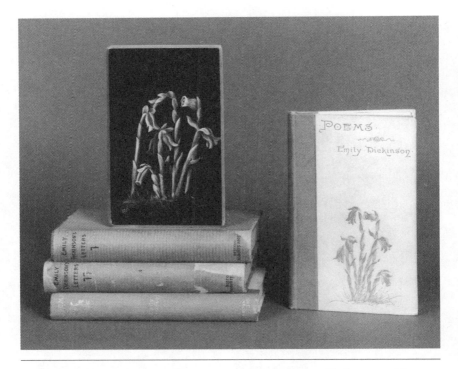

Mabel's painting of Indian pipes. Courtesy of the Folger Shakespeare Library, Washington, D.C., and the Amherst College Archives and Special Collections.

ferred flower of life, seems almost supernatural, and the sweet glee that I felt at meeting it, I could confide to none. I still cherish the clutch with which I bore it from the ground when a wondering Child, an unearthly booty, and maturity only enhances mystery, never decreases it." [22] Indian pipes appear in Emily's herbarium, collected forty years before. She collected it on her woodland walks. Referring to a sprig of witch hazel that her cousins sent, Emily said, "I had never seen it but once before, and it haunted me like childhood's Indian pipe, or ecstatic puff-balls, or that mysterious apple that sometimes comes on river-pinks." [23]

Emily was like Indian pipes. She relied on family members—first her father, then Vinnie—for major exchanges with the outside world: necessities, protection and news. She traded back letters and poems. A month after receiving the painted panel, she wrote to Mabel, "I cannot

---

→| INDIAN PIPE |←

The Indian pipe (*Monotropa uniflora*) is an unusual plant, visually and botanically. It looks like a waxy albino stem of lily of the valley, completely white and leafless. In my shade garden, it pops up in small groups in August in leaf litter around the roots of the Norway spruce. The flowers nod to the ground, a nod to its genus, *Mono-tropa,* as well, Greek for "one turn."

Native to the Northeast, it is an angiosperm, a flowering plant, but one incapable of photosynthesis. Unlike the green growing things around it, it can't manufacture its own food but relies on symbiotic relationships. A special fungus called mycorrhiza sends nutrients like nitrogen and phosphorus to the roots of larger plants, often oaks or conifers. In exchange, the fungus sends food from the tree roots to the Indian pipes. It is botanical barter at its best.

---

make an Indian Pipe but please accept a Humming Bird" [24] and enclosed the poem "A Route of Evanescence."

If not for a twist in the plot, after the episode of the Indian pipes Mabel Todd would be a footnote in the pages of the Emily Dickinson annals. She and Austin Dickinson became lovers.

Austin and Mabel? They seemed an unlikely couple. Both married and twenty-seven years apart in age, it was an autumn-spring romance. They first "declared" in 1882, on one of their many long drives around the Amherst countryside. Mabel says of Austin, "He was as much a poet as she [Emily]. Only his genius did not flower in verse or rhyme, but rather in an intense and cultivated knowledge of nature, in a passionate joy in the landscapes to be seen from many a hilltop near Amherst, and in the multitude of trees and blossoming shrubs all about him." [25] He excused himself to Mabel one day, driving off to supervise the digging of a tree for installation on the college campus. "I don't like to trust anyone with an oak," he said.²⁶

Their relationship flowered in secret, but became widely known. There's nothing like a small town to brew a scandal that's downright operatic. Austin cut a road through the Dickinson meadow and gave the Todds a building lot, helping them site and landscape their new home. You can still see "The Dell," an elaborate Queen Anne cottage with its arched front porch, just a block from the Evergreens. Unfortunately its shingles are no longer painted red with green trim, the colors that Mabel chose. The square stone posts that Austin used to mark the new road are at the east end of Spring Street.

The Dickinson sisters accepted the couple, and as you might imagine, were estranged from Susan. Mutton-chopped Austin and ringleted Mabel often met at the Homestead's parlor or piazza. Imagine them sitting on summer evenings, their chairs arranged among the potted plants. Strolling in the garden, the smell of the honeysuckle wafted over from the trellis. As dusk fell, the flower beds caught the ebbing light.

Austin and Mabel's bond lasted. Neither divorced; their relationship ended only with Austin's death in 1895.

"Thy Daisy Draped for Thee"

Emily also had deep friendships with men, but speculation regarding her love life tends more to gossip than proof. With sketchy evidence, biographers have pointed to (among others) Charles Wadsworth, a friend and minister, and Samuel Bowles, the editor of the *Springfield Republican*, as the inspiration for Emily's poems and letters about love. It is the lore of a broken heart, which always seemed to be the story; for any nineteenth-century woman who didn't marry, she must have been disappointed in affairs of the heart.

Late in life Emily had one substantiated love: Otis Phillips Lord, a longtime family friend. "Phil" was a retired judge of the Massachusetts Supreme Court, a staunch Whig like Emily's father, and by 1877, a widower. He called her "Daisy." A photograph from 1883 shows him sitting in his garden in Salem.

Thy flower - be gay -
Her Lord - away!
It ill becometh me -
I'll dwell in Calyx - Gray -
How modestly - alway -
Thy Daisy -
Draped for thee!

(367)

This poem was written in 1862, earlier than scholars can verify Emily's relationship with Lord. Was it tongue-in-cheek playing on the name, or just a coincidence? If the latter, Emily must have been amused by it in later years.

She and Lord never married, though he clearly wanted her to, and she considered it. She wore his ring, with "Philip" engraved inside, but she never joined him. His nieces, who lived with him and stood to inherit his money, were clearly against it, referring to Emily as a "hussy." He died in 1884, another loss in a sad decade of Emily's life.

Winter in Emily Dickinson's Garden

In one of her poems, Emily reminds us that "Winter under cultivation / is arable as Spring." [27] Left in her garden, remnants of last year's plants insulate the crown of the plant, the growing area that will reemerge in the spring. There is nostalgia in a winter garden, but also hope.

Snow clings to the trees around the Homestead, glazing them into exquisite confections; there is a reason why bakers call cake decorations "icing" and "frosting." An old photograph shows the Homestead in winter with snow topping the hedge and large white pines in front of the house.

In some storms, precipitation is confused, sliding from liquid to solid. The temperature hovers around freezing. Tree branches are glazed and shimmer in the sun. Emily called it "winter's silver fracture."[28] Icicles, quick stalactites, form in the eaves of the Dickinson house and barn where water trickles down, tapering to a point. On the days when the ice melts, standing under the eaves can be a dangerous proposition.

Winter in Emily's garden is a time of trees. Oaks hold up their broad shoulders. Elms look like great vases. Maples are oval. Locusts are sinuous, snaky. In the bare branches, nests are revealed, birds' and squirrels'.

The trees with bark as their biggest asset finally get their turn at the podium. Beeches have silver trunks that look like elephants' skin. Paper birches, their bright white, curving bark brilliant against the evergreens, mock the snow. They exfoliate, the bark peeling off in thin sheets like leaves. The sycamores' bark flakes like old skin, leaving mottled trunks in white and grey and brown. Emily mentions it in the last stanza of this poem, comparing its brown to cinnamon or perhaps myrrh, that biblical gift of the Magi used to anoint the dead.

What care the Dead for Winter?
Themselves as easy freeze -
June Noon - as January Night -
As soon the South - her Breeze
Of Sycamore - or Cinnamon -
Deposit in a Stone
And put a Stone to keep it Warm -
Give Spices - unto Men -

(624)

The deciduous trees are elegant skeletons, sharp silhouettes against the sky. Their screen of leaves abandoned, they show off their mathematical structures.

Pruning cuts show in winter. Branches of fruit trees are regularly lopped off to strengthen the fruit buds or to open up the center of the tree, allowing more light for ripening next year's crop. Some of the fruit trees in Emily's winter garden look like young boys with bad haircuts, embarrassed by their heavy trimming. But over time, with regular pruning, they become sculptures.

Conifers supply the structure or bones of many winter gardens, and Emily's was no exception. "My garden is a little knoll with faces under it, and only the pines sing tunes, now the birds are absent." [29] The evergreen conifers of the Homestead's hemlock hedge make green walls and provide a backdrop for borders. They contrast with the snow.

Looking out her bedroom window, Emily saw a large white pine. More of them lined the drive and the path between the two houses. Emily sent this poem about a pine tree to her friend Samuel Bowles. She enclosed a sprig of white pine to be sure he could decode the riddle.

⌒

> A feather from the Whippowill
> That everlasting - sings!
> Whose galleries - are Sunrise -
> Whose Opera - the Springs -
> Whose Emerald Nest the Ages spin
> Of mellow - murmuring thread -
> Whose Beryl Egg, what School Boys hunt
> In "Recess -" Overhead!
>
>   (208A)

The soft, feathery needles of the white pine are bluish-green. If you pull some off a branch, you'll see that they grow in little bundles—"fascicles," like Emily's poems. When the wind blows, the pine does sing. Its new seed-bearing cones are the color of beryl, a pale sea-green gem. And things aren't that different now; schoolboys still like to climb trees and hunt pinecones during recess.

A huge white oak stands sentinel on the western side of the Homestead, outside Emily's father's study and what was her conservatory. In her day, it was a new tree, and scholars speculate that Austin planted it there. If so, he chose the site wisely, leaving space for the horizontal branches. Today it spreads over much of the lawn. It's likely that Austin transplanted the white oak sapling from the woods near Amherst, where it is a native denizen.

In earlier years, Emily strolled the same woods, collecting the oak's acorns.

⌒

I robbed the Woods -
The trusting Woods -
The unsuspecting Trees
Brought out their Burs and mosses
My fantasy to please -
I scanned their trinkets curious -
I grasped - I bore away -
What will the solemn Hemlock -
What will the Oak tree say?

(57A)

If you find one of the leaves from Emily's white oak, you will see that it is simply shaped, like a child's drawing. Its leaves are lobed. In winter, the dried leaves sometimes splinter, leaving only the outline and veins intact. During her life, an editor said that Emily's poems "remind[ed him] of skeleton leaves so pretty but *too delicate*,—not strong enough to publish." [30]

─────────────── ⇥ **PLANT HISTORY: OAK** ⇤ ───────────────

Oaks are ancient trees of Europe and North America, inhabited by the old gods. Zeus wasn't above occupying an oak, when the occasion arose. Nordic elders worshipped the deep roots and broad crowns, the underworld and heaven united. The name of the genus, *Quercus*, is thought to be from a Celtic word meaning "to inquire." It was among the oaks that the Druids most often made their ritual petitions.

But old religions yielded to imperialism, and the forests of Europe fell. Hardwooded oaks were prey to the architects of war and trade. Straight trunks morphed into masts and the elbows of branches into strong hulls. Builders domestic, scholastic, and ecclesiastic used oak to half-timber houses and vault halls. Small wonder that explorers in North America wrote back excitedly about the continent's towering specimens. They were followed by settlers who cut the oaks down and, eventually, homeowners like Austin Dickinson who replanted them.

Surviving the Winter

During the winter, apples and root crops like potatoes were kept in the cellar under the Homestead. Without refrigeration, except for an icebox with ice cut from the local pond, the Dickinsons relied on their cold, dry root cellar. They called it the hoarding-cellar. Its crates of potatoes, barrels of apples, and cabinets lined with jars of fruit carried their dinner table through the winter months.

⌒

Like Brooms of Steel
The Snow and Wind

Had swept the Winter Street -
The House was hooked
The Sun sent out
Faint Deputies of Heat -
Where rode the Bird
The Silence tied
His ample - plodding Steed
The Apple in the Cellar snug
Was all the one that played.

(1241)

Emily would have walked down the cellar steps to get a jar of preserves for the dining room, remembering the summer's crop in a tangible way. She would sometimes bring the key to the wine cellar with her, fetching a bottle of currant wine or Malmsey wine, a kind of Madeira that her mother preferred. Between the cellar windows at the front of the house was the cabinet where she cooled her newly baked gingerbread.

Prospecting for Summer

Gardeners know that winter is the season of plant and seed catalogues, drifting into the mailbox like so much snow. Catalogues fuel garden dreams with mouthwatering descriptions and luscious illustrations. The Dickinsons were not immune. A letter of 1881 has Emily describing Vinnie "in Bliss' Catalogue, prospecting for Summer."[31] Gold was discovered at Sutter's Mill in 1848, but it's easier to strike a

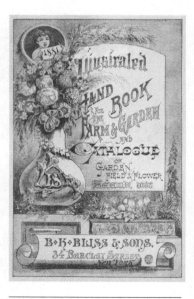

The Bliss catalogue

vein in a flower catalogue, if a bit more expensive to the winter gardener's budget.

The Bliss catalogue was bliss to any gardener with spring fever, a weighty book of 141 pages plus supplement. It was one of the original mail-order seed businesses in America. B. K. Bliss (eventually "& Sons") was located first in Springfield, Massachusetts, then in New York City. Bliss printed the first catalogue with color plates in 1853 and introduced many new varieties of vegetables and flowers into American gardens, including Emily's. It featured engravings with that come-hither look and a full-color page of pansies guaranteed to send any gardener for a checkbook. Of course, in those days, remittances could also have been in the form of postage stamps.

Gardeners' favorite catalogue choices are often the rare and exotic. The gardener acquires bragging rights; there's nothing better than having the first specimen of a unique variety. Then, as now, imports were trendy. Austin, for example, planted many Norway spruce trees (*Picea abies*) around the Evergreens. One of Emily's poems describes this man-made movement of plants.

As if some little Arctic flower
Opon the polar hem -
Went wandering down the Latitudes
Until it puzzled came
To continents of summer -
To firmaments of sun -
To strange, bright crowds of flowers -
And birds, of foreign tongue!
I say, As if this little flower
To Eden, wandered in -
What then? Why nothing,
Only, your *inference* therefrom!

(177)

A Winter Garden Primer

Emily also prospected for summer with the plants in her conservatory. Daphne bloomed, tiny clusters of white flowers, sweetly fragrant. Emily described daphne as "a more civic Arbutus." Reconsidering, she said, "[T]he suggestion is invidious, for are not both as beautiful as Delight can make them?" [32]

Potted hyacinths for filling a window

Indoor bulbs gave winter rewards. In a letter to her cousins, Emily wrote, "I have made a permanent Rainbow by filling a Window with Hyacinths, which Science will be glad to know, and have a Cargo of Carnations, worthy of Ceylon." [33] Mattie associated the scent of hyacinths with Emily's room in winter, "for the way of a bulb in the sunshine had an uncanny fascination for her, their little pots crowding all four window-sills to bring a reluctant spring upon the air." [34] You can easily create your own permanent rainbow by forcing your own bulbs.

How to Force Bulbs

Forcing bulbs is a process of adjusting and controlling light and temperature. You create an artificial spring, inducing bloom. It's easier than it sounds.

If you've never forced a bulb, start with paperwhite narcissus. They are synonymous with instant gratification. You will find them in any garden center around Christmastime. Select firm bulbs with their skin intact, the same way you would pick an onion. Stick them, roots down, in a container lined with about an inch of pebbles. Water to the depth of the pebbles, and stand back. You'll be rewarded with leaves within a week and flowers in a month or two.

To vary the effect, use beach glass, river rocks, or aquarium gravel instead of pebbles. Or find funky containers. Try a martini glass with grey polished rocks to start a single bulb. The roots will be visible, which adds interest, and the flare of the glass contrasts nicely with the upright habit of the bulb.

The only word of caution on paperwhites is that they have an extraordinary smell. It is sweet and spicy but not to everyone's taste. After they've bloomed, toss them on your compost pile. They're used up and won't bloom again.

Slightly more work, but quite rewarding, are hardy bulbs that normally bloom year after year outdoors, like Emily's daffodils or crocus. Hardy bulbs are like friends who need a little more encouragement to blossom. Here's how to force them:

1. Pick your varieties. If you are ordering from a catalogue, look for the words "easy forcer" or "early bloom."

2. If you are picking out the bulbs in person, select the largest bulbs you can find. The bigger the bulb, the bigger the bloom.

3. Pot the bulbs in sterile potting mix. A bag of potting mix that you buy at a garden center has been superheated to sterilize it and generally includes soil, peat moss, and vermiculite or perlite. Place the growing tip of the bulb about an inch below the surface of the soil. Space the bulbs at least half an inch apart. Use pots that have drainage holes.

4. Water the pots well, letting the water drain out of the holes.

5. Place the pots in a cool, dark area: refrigerator, storm cellar stairs, an attached but unheated garage or attic. Emily probably put her bulbs in the root cellar. The trick is to chill the bulbs but not freeze them. Figure on about twelve weeks of cold. This process is called "vernalization,"

the process of exposing bulbs, seeds, or plants to the cold, imitating the conditions they would have had outside.

6. Check the pots once a week, and water if dry.

7. Eventually, leaves will pop out of the top of the bulbs. Because they have been in the dark, the leaves will be white or yellowish. Move the pots to a brightly lit window. Use a cool room if possible. The lower temperature will keep the foliage and flower stems compact, avoiding horticultural sprawl.

8. Enjoy the blooms!

With the exception of tulips, hardy bulbs can be replanted outside. Let the foliage yellow and die, and plant in early summer. Give them a shot of bulb fertilizer in the fall. You may not see bloom the next year, but by the second year, the flowers will be back.

If you force your own bulbs, you may want to start with that favorite of Emily, hyacinths. One March, she wrote to a friend, "I wish I could show you the Hyacinths that embarrass us by their loveliness, though to cower before a flower is perhaps unwise - but Beauty is often timidity - perhaps oftener - pain." [35] Even though she may have cowered before the beauty of the blooms, she was never timid about growing them.

According to Scott Kunst, proprietor of Old House Garden Bulbs, Emily probably would have forced regular hyacinths, as opposed to Roman hyacinths or grape hyacinths. It's likely that Emily would have used a forcing glass for her hyacinths. If you want to own a period piece, it will cost upwards of $200. But reproductions, "new heirlooms," are much cheaper. (See the Resources.)

Even with growing things indoors and ordering plants for next year's garden, the season drags. But winter can be a time of reflection, for gardeners and poets.

Winter is good - his Hoar Delights
Italic flavor yield -
To Intellects inebriate
With Summer, or the World -

Generic as a Quarry
And hearty - as a Rose -
Invited with asperity
But welcome when he goes.

(1374)

As the days get longer, the snows don't last. Emily called them "transient." Spring is coming. Looking out her window, Emily stood witness to the seasons in her garden, her "ribbons of the year." [36] Whatever the season, her garden was inspiration for her poems. And her poems have proved perennial indeed.

The Angle of a Landscape -
That every time I wake -
Between my Curtain and the Wall
Opon an ample Crack -

Like a Venetian - waiting -
Accosts my open eye -
Is just a Bough of Apples -
Held slanting, in the Sky -

The Pattern of a Chimney -
The Forehead of a Hill -
Sometimes - a Vane's Forefinger -
But that's - Occasional -

The Seasons - shift - my Picture -
Opon my Emerald Bough,
I wake - to find no - Emeralds
Then - Diamonds - which the Snow

From Polar Caskets - fetched me -
The Chimney - and the Hill -
And just the Steeple's finger -
These - never stir at all -

(578)

$\mathcal{E}$mily died in May 1886, succumbing to what the doctor diagnosed as Bright's disease, a kidney ailment. Her funeral was held in the Homestead parlor on May 19. Emily was laid out dressed in white, with violets and a pink cypripedium orchid at her throat. Vinnie placed two heliotropes by her hand to take to Judge Lord. Susan arranged violets and ground pine on her white casket. After the service, the Dickinsons' Irish workmen lifted the casket. They carried it out from the back of the house and through the garden. It was a brilliant spring afternoon. Apple-blossoms festooned the trees. Mabel Todd remembered, "Then we all walked quietly across the sunny fields, full of innocents & buttercups to the cemetery."[1]

Visiting West Cemetery, you can still see Emily Dickinson's grave in the family plot. The original gravestone is gone, the new one placed there by her niece Mattie. In any season, even on frozen ground, you will often find a flower left by an admirer.

A Poet's Legacy

Emily had charged Vinnie with destroying her papers. Put yourself in Vinnie's shoes: she is sitting in her older sister's empty bedroom, no doubt at the well-used writing table. She opens the drawers of the cherry chest and pulls out stacks of clippings, decades of letters from friends and family, and sadly, following her sister's wishes, wistfully puts them aside. Later she burns them. But then she finds something odd—a box filled with small, hand-sewn booklets. About forty "volumes." Hundreds and hundreds of poems. Thankfully for us, she can't bear to get rid of them.

Scholars call these booklets "fascicles." Fittingly, *fascicle* is also a botanical term for a cluster of leaves or flowers or roots growing together from a base. Emily's work, the careful copying, ordering and binding, and her small notations—she put small cross marks to footnote choices of several words—was like her herbarium, carefully arranged and labeled. "In childhood I never sowed a seed unless it was perennial - and that is why my garden lasts," she wrote.[2]

TWO SISTERS, A HEDGE APART

After Emily's death, Vinnie lived alone in the Homestead for another thirteen years until her death in August 1899. She continued to tend Emily's garden. Pulled in a tug-of-war that started over Austin and continued with Emily's posthumous fame, she quarreled with both Mabel Loomis Todd and with Susan. Vinnie eventually sued Mabel over a strip of the Dickinson meadow adjacent to the Todd house, giving more fuel to the small-town gossips. With Susan it was sometimes pettier, though maybe not from a gardener's point of view.

Every fall, Vinnie had Emily's shrubs and rosebushes top-dressed with well-rotted manure from the barn. One year, when arranging this job, the hired man told her that Susan had used all of the "dressing" on her flowerbeds. A friend found Vinnie so angry, she was having heart palpitations. A fight over a manure pile? Only a gardener could appreciate the true value of this composted black gold.

With what she later called her "Joan of Arc feeling," [3] Vinnie brought Emily's poems first to Susan, who chose to send them out one at a time to periodicals. It was too slow for Vinnie. Recovering them from the Evergreens, Vinnie marched across Main Street to the Dell, to Mabel Loomis Todd. Mabel took up the banner, convincing none other than Thomas Wentworth Higginson that they were worthy of publication. Mabel spent days, hours, years deciphering Emily's poems and letters, transcribing the spidery script with an ancient typewriter. It's no surprise that Mabel's Indian pipes grace the front cover of the first edition of Emily's poems.

Emily was always ambivalent about publishing. "Publication - is the Auction / Of the Mind of Man -" is the opening to one of her poems. [4] With a wintry allusion, she continues, "but We - would rather / From Our Garret go / White - unto the White Creator- / Than invest - Our Snow -" She invested her snow, her poems, by cherishing them in a cherry chest, waiting for a new season of a sister and a friend to see them into print.

A Gardener's Legacy

Unlike her poems, Emily's gardens fell on hard times after Vinnie's death.

The Homestead passed out of the Dickinson family, and new owners grassed over much of Emily's garden, adding terraces and formal flower beds in the style of the day. They installed a tennis court at the far corner of the property. In the same fit of renovation, they removed the barn, along with Mrs. Dickinson's cherished figs. To give the Homestead a more trendy colonial revival look, they sandblasted the original cream-colored paint from the brick.

Saddest of all, demolition claimed Emily's conservatory. A palimpsest of it is still vaguely visible on the exterior brick. If you walk around the back of the new garage, you can see the conservatory windows, reused in an architectural demonstration of Yankee thrift.

The hemlock hedge has grown into a row of trees, and the fence with its gates and latches is gone. Only a few of the trees that her father and brother planted on the property still stand.

An aberrant hurricane tore through Amherst in 1938, a storm of Biblical proportions. This meteorological explosion turned Amherst's tree-lined streets into a maze of fallen trunks. A newspaper account says that the town lost thousands of trees. The journalist wrote of the particular vengeance on the Dickinson land. Over a hundred trees came down between the Homestead and the Evergreens. Emily's pine trees were all lost. "Four black walnut trees, a rarity in this section, went down, as well as oaks, maples, spruces, pines, elms, one grand tulip tree and some hickory. These properties probably lost more of value [than] any other one private holding." [5] Luckily, the oak still stood.

Emily was clairvoyant when she wrote this poem sixty years earlier:

The Wind took up the Northern Things
And piled them in the South -
Then gave the East unto the West
And opening his mouth
The four Divisions of the Earth
Did make as to devour
While everything to corners slunk
Behind the awful power -

The Wind unto his Chamber went
And nature ventured out -
Her subjects scattered into place
Her systems ranged about

Again the smoke from Dwellings rose
The Day abroad was heard
How intimate, a Tempest past
The Transport of the Bird -

(1152)

The Dickinson Homestead is now owned by Amherst College and is open to the public. The College has been kind to the garden, slowly bringing it back to something Emily would recognize. The tennis court is gone. The remaining trees are well-tended. In 1972, the Trustees asked William I. P. Campbell, Horticulturist Emeritus at Smith College, to advise on a reconstruction of the garden. To pick the plants, he used references in her poems, studied her herbarium, and researched in period catalogues. Subsequent Homestead gardeners have maintained and enhanced Campbell's designs. The gardens would be different to Emily, but delightful.

In recent years, the groundwork has been laid for more extensive projects to preserve and restore the Homestead and Evergreen landscapes. Amherst College has acquired the Evergreens from the Martha Dickinson Bianchi Trust, consolidating the properties under one entity, the Emily Dickinson Museum. A graduate student spent a semester

The gardens at the Dickinson Homestead today

researching the Dickinson fence, measuring remnants that are in stor-age, analyzing the paint, and making scale drawings so that some future craftsman can re-create it. A historian, Rudy Favretti, documented the landscape in a report for the Homestead. New plantings are calling back the garden of Emily's day, like the Clapp's Favorite pear tree that was planted along the flagstone path.

Today, Emily could pick out remnants of her garden, the way an archaeologist spots original shards in a restored vessel. The granite steps and flagstones still lead down to the garden beds. Peonies still poke their red noses through the soil in spring. Lilacs, ancient shrubs, bloom every year. And the last time I visited, two hummingbirds buzzed, obliv-ious to metaphor but still making their evanescent route around the garden.

RESOURCES

*I*f you want to grow the flowers that Emily grew, you will need to do some mail-order shopping, either via the Internet or on paper. Heirloom plants are often not available at your local nursery. Make a list, and hold onto your pocketbook. Prospecting for summer can be addictive.

ANTIQUE ROSE EMPORIUM
9300 Lueckmeyer Road
Brenham, TX 77833
(800) 441-0002
www.antiqueroseemporium.com
To find Emily's damask maid, go to the Antique Rose Emporium. It specializes in old garden roses and has a lovely website to boot.

ARROWHEAD ALPINES
P.O. Box 857
1310 N. Gregory Road
Fowlerville, MI 48836
(517) 223-3581
www.arrowhead-alpines.com

Many of the wildflowers that Emily collected for her herbarium are prop-agated by Arrowhead Alpines and available for your woodland garden. By growing these plants, you will be protecting the genetic diversity of Emily's time and our own.

Brent and Becky's Bulbs
7463 Heath Trail
Gloucester, VA 23061
(877) 661-2852
www.brentandbeckysbulbs.com
Brent and Becky Heath are knowledgeable and reliable suppliers of high-quality bulbs. While not all of their varieties are heirloom, their catalogue notes the difference.

W. Atlee Burpee & Co.
300 Park Avenue
Warminster, PA 18991-0003
(800) 888-1447
The granddaddy of American seed companies, Burpee also sells garden supplies and some plants.

Completely Clematis
217 Argilla Road
Ipswich, MA 01938-2617
(978) 356-3197
www.clematisnursery.com
If your trellis is hankering for a vine with an electric curl, what better place to order it than Completely Clematis?

Cook's Garden
P.O. Box 65
Londonderry, VT 05148
(802) 824-3400
www.cooksgarden.com

Heirloom and specialty seeds for the culinary and cutting gardens. Their catalogue is illustrated New Englandly, with lovely woodcuts.

EDIBLE LANDSCAPING
P.O. Box 77
Afton, VA 22920
(800) 524-4156
www.eat-it.com
For Mrs. Dickinson's Brown Turkey figs.

FAIRWEATHER GARDENS
P.O. Box 330
Greenwich, NJ 08323
(856) 451-6261
www.fairweathergardens.com
Robert Hoffman and Robert Popham search the world for unusual varieties of shrubs, trees, and perennials. Some are vintage and some new, but all choice. Fairweather Gardens is for a gardener like Austin Dickinson who values the exotic.

FORESTFARM
990 Tetherow Rd.
Williams, OR 97544-9599
(541) 846-7269
www.forestfarm.com
Unusual perennials are available from Forestfarm. Try their tubes. The plants that arrive at your doorstep will seem puny, but their roots systems are robust.

LOGEE'S GREENHOUSES, LTD.
141 North Street
Danielson, CT 06239-1939
(888) 330-8038
www.logees.com

Emily and Vinnie would have loved this catalogue. It offers a wide sampling of rare and unusual flowering plants for home, the garden, and the conservatory.

Old House Gardens—Heirloom Bulbs

536 Third Street

Ann Arbor, MI 48103

(734) 995-1486

www.oldhousegardens.com

For the best selection of heirloom bulbs in the country, tiptoe through the Old House Gardens catalogue. Choices include a bulb collection called "Forcing for Beginners" and a hyacinth vase reproduced from an 1850s original. The proprietor, Scott Kunst, is knowledgeable and responsive, not to mention funny. An English major, he is also an Emily Dickinson fan. Don't miss his e-mail newsletters.

Perennial Pleasures Nursery

P.O. Box 147

East Hardwick, VT 05836

(802) 472-5104

www.perennialpleasures.net

When I was looking to grow unusual annuals like four-o'clocks and mignonette that Emily had in her garden, I turned to Rachel Kane at Perennial Pleasures Nursery in Vermont. A specialist in heritage plants, she sent me well-grown and carefully shipped six-packs that quickly established in my garden. As the name indicates, she specializes in perennials but also carries a large selection of herbs and heritage annuals.

RareFind Nursery

957 Patterson Road

Jackson, NJ 08527

(732) 833-0613

www.rarefindnursery.com

Austin Dickinson loved rhododendron, and so does Hank Schannen, the proprietor of this specialty grower. RareFind, as the name suggests, concentrates on the uncommon, and as a result you'll often find offerings of forgotten older varieties of plants. If you are driving past Jackson, New Jersey, give yourself a treat and stop by their eleven-acre "gardenesque" nursery.

SEED SAVERS EXCHANGE
3076 North Winn Road
Decorah, IA 52101
(563) 382-5990
www.seedsavers.org
A nonprofit organization founded in 1975 to help save heirloom seeds.

SELECT SEEDS—ANTIQUE FLOWERS
180 Stickney Hill Road
Union, CT 06076
(860) 684-9310
www.selectseeds.com
Their motto is bringing "the flowers our grandmothers loved into our gardens once more." With more than a hundred varieties of perennials and annuals from the days before the twentieth century, they have seeds and plants for many of the varieties that Emily loved. Select Seeds specializes in "open-pollinated" varieties that reproduce true to type. These contrast with hybrids that are either sterile or whose offspring look suspiciously unlike their parents—the botanical equivalent of the milkman.

THOMPSON & MORGAN
P.O. Box 1308
Jackson, NJ 08527
(800) 274-7333
An English seedsman, located in South Jersey. Go figure! Large selection of cultivars.

White Flower Farm
P.O. Box 50
Route 63
Litchfield, CT 06759
(800) 503-9624
www.whiteflowerfarm.com
The White Flower Farm catalogue is an education, an entertainment, and a seduction. With mouthwatering photographs, common names, scientific names, and pronunciation, you can create your own course in perennial plant identification. Warning, you'll want one (or three) of each. Also a great source for flowering shrubs and red-nosed peonies.

Womenswork
Little Big Farm
P.O. Box 543
York, ME 03909
800-639-2709
If you don't have hired help like the Dickinsons, you can order the best goatskin garden gloves, bar none, from Womenswork. They have other fun tools too.

NOTES

*U*nless otherwise stated, quotations from Emily Dickinson's poems are from *The Complete Poems of Emily Dickinson*, ed. Ralph W. Franklin (Cambridge: Belknap Press of Harvard University Press, 1998). Quotations from the poems are cited here using the abbreviation *P*, followed by the poem number.

CHAPTER 1: *Early Spring*

1. Martha Dickinson Bianchi, *Emily Dickinson Face to Face*. Boston: Houghton Mifflin, 1932: 39.

2. Edward Dickinson to Emily Norcross, 27 June 1827, *A Poet's Parents*, ed. Vivian Pollack. Chapel Hill: The University of North Carolina Press, 1988: 114.

3. *The Letters of Emily Dickinson*, eds. Thomas H. Johnson and Theodora Ward. Cambridge: Belknap Press of Harvard University Press, 1958: 206. Unless otherwise stated, quotations from Emily Dickinson's letters are cited using the abbreviation *L*, followed by the letter number.

4. *L*, 52.

5. *L*, 206.

6. *L*, 129.

7. *L*, 339.

8. *L*, 976.

9. *P*, 16.

10. *L*, 885.

11. *L*, 435.

12. *Emily Dickinson Face to Face*, 39.

13. *L*, 206.

14. MacGregor Jenkins, *Emily Dickinson: Friend and Neighbor*. Boston: Little, Brown, 1939: 121.

CHAPTER 2: *Late Spring*

1. *L*, 122.

2. *L*, 2.

3. *L*, 3.

4. Jay Leyda, *The Years and Hours of Emily Dickinson*. New Haven: Yale University Press, 1960: I: 84.

5. *L*, 488.

6. Mrs. Almira H. Lincoln, *Familiar Lectures on Botany*. Hartford: H. and F. J. Huntington, 12.

7. Andrea DiNoto and David Winter, *The Pressed Plant*. New York: Stewart, Tabori and Chang, 1999: 71.

8. *L*, 6.

9. The list of plants in Emily Dickinson's herbarium in Harvard University's Houghton Library was compiled by Edward L. Davis, Professor of Botany at the University of Massachusetts (undated), and amended by Ray Angelo, Curator of Vascular Plants for the New England Botanical Club in February 1984. Both are stored in the herbarium file in Houghton's archives (Am1118.11). Another source with a well-researched list of plants on the Dickinson property is Guy Leighton's master's thesis, "The Emily Dickinson Homestead" (University of Massachusetts, Amherst: Department of Landscape Architecture and Regional Planning, 1978). A copy of this thesis is in the Jones Library's Emily Dickinson Room in Amherst.

10. *P*, 1261.

11. *L*, 117.

12. *L*, 492.

13. *L*, 271.

14. *P*, 280.

15. *L*, 261.

16. *L*, 233.

17. *L*, 212.

18. *The Years and Hours of Emily Dickinson*, II: 21.

19. *L*, 314.

20. *L*, 319.

21. *L*, 23.

22. *L*, 339.

23. Amos Eaton, *Manual of Botany*. Albany: Websters and Skinners, 1822: 446.

24. *L*, 318.

25. Polly Longsworth, *A Poet's Parents*. Chapel Hill: The University of North Carolina Press, 1988: 210.

26. *Emily Dickinson Face to Face*, 4.

27. Ibid., 5.

28. Millicent Todd Bingham, *Emily Dickinson's Home*. New York: Harper & Brothers, 1955, 239.

29. *L*, 691.

30. *P*, 29.

31. *L*, 340.

32. *L*, 262.

33. *L*, 823.

34. *L*, 92.

35. *L*, 163.

36. *L*, 499.

37. *P*, 1547.

38. *L*, 502.

39. *P*, 1426.

40. *L*, 23.

CHAPTER 3: *Early Summer*

1. *L*, 318.

2. *L*, 13

3. *Transactions of the Massachusetts Horticultural Society for the Years 1843-4-5-6.* Boston: Dutton and Wentworth's Print, 1847: 158.

4. *L*, 13.

5. *L*, 17.

6. *L*, 178.

7. *L*, 178.

8. *L*, 182.

9. *L*, 182.

10. *Emily Dickinson Face to Face*, 25.

11. *Emily Dickinson: Friend and Neighbor*, 91.

12. *L*, 165.

13. *L*, 267.

14. *L*, 820.

15. Martha Dickinson Bianchi, published in *Emily Dickinson International Society (EDIS) Bulletin*, Nov/Dec 1990, ed. Barton Levi St. Armand. Vol. 2, no. 2: 1–3. Mattie wrote this richly descriptive essay entitled "Emily Dickinson's Garden" and read it October 14, 1936, at the Garden Club of Arlington, Massachusetts.

16. *L*, 235.

17. *Emily Dickinson: Friend and Neighbor*, 13.

18. Martha Dickinson Bianchi, published in *Emily Dickinson International Society (EDIS) Bulletin*, Nov/Dec 1990, ed. Barton Levi St. Armand. Vol. 2, no. 2: 1–3.

19. *L*, 308.

20. *L*, 904.

21. *The Selected Writings of Ralph Waldo Emerson*, ed. Brooks Atkinson. New York: The Modern Library, Random House, 1992: 299.

22. *L*, 472.

23. George Frisbie Whicher, *Emily Dickinson: This was a Poet.* New York: Charles Scribner's Sons, 1938: 55.

24. *L*, 888.

25. *L*, 1038.

CHAPTER 4: *Late Summer*

1. *L*, 650.

2. *L*, 235.

3. *Complete Poems of Emily Dickinson*, ed. Martha Dickinson Bianchi. Boston: Little, Brown and Company, 1924: Introduction.

4. *L*, 330.

5. *L*, 260.

6. *L*, 342a.

7. *L*, 342b.

8. Polly Longsworth, *The Dickinsons of Amherst.* Hanover, NH: The University of New England Press, 1991: 40.

9. *L*, 271.

10. *L*, 1002.

11. Martha Dickinson Bianchi, *The Life and Letters of Emily Dickinson.* Boston: Houghton Mifflin, 1924: 53.

12. *L*, 279.

13. *L*, 437.

14. *Emily Dickinson Face to Face*, 4.

15. *Emily Dickinson: Friend and Neighbor*, 122.

16. *L*, 315.

17. *Emily Dickinson Face to Face*, 42.

18. *L*, 969.

19. *Emily Dickinson International Society (EDIS) Bulletin*, Nov/Dec 1990, ed. Barton Levi St. Armand. Vol. 2, no. 2: 1–3.

20. *P*, 5.

21. *Emily Dickinson: Friend and Neighbor*, 36.

22. *Emily Dickinson Face to Face*, 136.

23. *L*, 771.

24. *L*, 262.

25. *L*, 851.

26. *L*, 711.

27. *Emily Dickinson: Face to Face*, 9.

28. *Emily Dickinson: Friend and Neighbor*, 21.

29. Ibid., 41.

30. Ibid., 37.

31. Ibid., 58.

32. Martha Dickinson Bianchi, *Recollections of a Country Girl*, 1935. An unpublished manuscript in the archives of the Brown University Library, Martha Dickinson Bianchi Papers D-B-H 10:18, 10:19, 292.

33. *L*, 502.

34. *L*, 473.

35. *L*, 723.

36. *L*, 272.

37. *Emily Dickinson: Friend and Neighbor*, 73.

38. *L*, 308.

39. Mary Adele Allen, *Around a Village Green*. Northampton, Mass., 1939: 76.

40. *L*, 1004.

41. *L*, 267.

42. *L*, 267.

43. *L*, 195.

44. *L*, 405a.

45. *Emily Dickinson Face to Face*, 9.

46. *L*, 49.

47. *Emily Dickinson International Society (EDIS) Bulletin*, Nov/Dec 1990, ed. Barton Levi St. Armand. Vol. 2, no. 2: 1–3.

48. Ibid.

49. *L*, 340.

50. *L*, 340.

51. *L*, 888.

52. *The Years and Hours of Emily Dickinson*, I: 207.

53. *L*, 195.

CHAPTER 5: *Autumn*

1. *L*, 7; 73.

2. *L*, 294.

3. *L*, 302.

4. *Recollections of a Country Girl*, 59.

5. Ibid., 17.

6. *The Years and Hours of Emily Dickinson*, II: 349.

7. *Recollections of a Country Girl*, 29.

8. *The Years and Hours of Emily Dickinson*, II: 30.

9. *L*, 668.

10. *The Years and Hours of Emily Dickinson*, I: 74.

11. Ibid., I: 129.

12. Ibid., I: 374.

13. *L*, 619.

14. *L*, 520.

15. *L*, 354.

16. *L*, 521.

17. *L*, 337.

18. *L*, 194.

19. *L*, 209.

20. *Emily Dickinson International Society (EDIS) Bulletin*, Vol. 2, no. 2 Nov/Dec 1990, ed. Barton Levi St. Armand, 1–3.

21. Ibid.

22. *L*, 268.

23. *L*, 1041.

24. *L*, 272.

25. *L*, 53.

26. *The Years and Hours of Emily Dickinson*, I: 359.

27. *L*, 656.

28. *L*, 53.

29. *L*, 1049.

30. *L*, 936.

31. *L*, 438.

32. *L*, 321.

33. *L*, 343.

34. *The Years and Hours of Emily Dickinson*, II: 381

35. *The Poetical Works of William Cullen Bryant*, ed. Parke Godwin. New York: D. Appleton & Company, 1883. II: 146.

36. *Bartlett's Familiar Quotations*, ed. Justin Kaplan (17th edition). Boston: Little, Brown, & Company, 2002. 318: 3. The Seasons. Autumn [1730], l.1.

37. *L*, 948.

38. *L*, 948.

39. *L*, 479.

40. *L*, 479.

41. *L*, 318.

42. *L*, 746.

43. *L*, 685.

44. *L*, 668.

CHAPTER 6: *Winter*

1. *L*, 190.

2. *L*, 9.

3. *L*, 212.

4. *L*, 432.

5. *L*, 735.

6. Millicent Todd Bingham, *Ancestor's Brocades*. New York: Harper & Brothers, 1945: 8.

7. *L*, 901.

8. *L*, 207.

9. Deborah Fiske to Helen Maria Fiske, October 4, 1841, from the Special Collections of Tutt Library, Colorado College, Colorado Springs, Colorado.

10. Nathan Fiske to Helen Maria Fiske, June 1, 1846, from the Special Collections of Tutt Library, Colorado College, Colorado Springs, Colorado.

11. *The Years and Hours of Emily Dickinson*, II: 14.

12. Helen Jackson, *Sonnets and Lyrics*. Boston: Roberts Brothers, 1886. Found on the internet at http://theotherpages.org/poems/hhj01.html.

13. *L*, 444a.

14. *L*, 601a.

15. *P*, 1488.

16. *L*, 602.

17. For a wonderful discussion of *Mercy Philbrick's Choice* and its author's relationship with Emily Dickinson, read the new biography by Kate Phillips, *Helen Hunt Jackson: A Literary Life*. Berkeley: University of California Press, 2003.

18. Helen Hunt Jackson, *Mercy Philbrick's Choice*. Boston: Roberts Brothers, 1876: 26.

19. Ibid., 125.

20. Ibid., 126.

21. *The Years and Hours of Emily Dickinson*, II: 361.

22. *L*, 769.

23. *L*, 479.

24. *L*, 770.

25. *Ancestor's Brocades*, 6.

26. Polly Longsworth, *Austin and Mabel*. New York: Farrar, Straus, Giroux, 1984: 118.

27. *P*, 1720.

28. *P*, 950.

29. *L*, 212.

30. Alfred Habegger, *My Wars Are Laid Away in Books: The Life of Emily Dickinson*. New York: Random House, 2001: 558.

31. *L*, 689.

32. *L*, 1037.

33. *L*, 882.

34. *Emily Dickinson Face to Face*, 45.

35. *L*, 807.

36. *P*, 1065.

Afterword

1. *Ancestor's Brocades*, 3.

2. *L*, 989.

3. *Ancestor's Brocades*, 87.

4. *P*, 788.

5. Newspaper article dated October 1, 1938, but without a title banner, from the Jones Library Special Collections lateral file.

Literary Credits

Emily Dickinson's poems are reprinted by permission of the publishers and the Trustees of Amherst College from *The Poems of Emily Dickinson*, Ralph W. Franklin, ed., Cambridge, Mass.: The Belknap Press of Harvard University Press, Copyright © 1998 by the President and Fellows of Harvard College. Copyright © 1951, 1955, 1979 by the President and Fellows of Harvard College.

Excerpts from Emily Dickinson's letters are reprinted by permission of the publishers from *The Letters of Emily Dickinson*, Thomas H. Johnson, ed., Cambridge, Mass.: The Belknap Press of Harvard University Press, Copyright © 1958, 1986 by the President and Fellows of Harvard College.

Photographic Credits

Unless otherwise noted, vintage etchings are from the author's collection.

PAGE 2: Emily Dickinson daguerreotype, by William C. North: Amherst College Archives and Special Collections. By permission of the Trustees of Amherst College.

PAGE 6: Homestead Lithograph by Bachelder, 1855: Courtesy of the Jones Library, Inc., Amherst, Mass.

PAGE 7: Conjectural Site Plan of the Homestead Property: the author.

PAGE 9: Edward Dickinson by Otis A. Bullard, early 1840: By permission of the Houghton Library, Harvard University (*MS AM 1118.9b Series II (79) & 84* and *MS Am 1118.11*).

PAGE 9: Emily Norcross Dickinson by Otis A. Bullard, early 1840: By permission of the Houghton Library, Harvard University (*MS AM 1118.9b Series II (79) & 84* and *MS Am 1118.11*).

PAGE 10: The Dickinson children by Otis A. Bullard, early 1840: By permission of the Houghton Library, Harvard University (*MS AM 1118.9b Series II (79) & 84* and *MS Am 1118.11*).

PAGE 23: Title page, Mrs. Almira H. Lincoln's *Familiar Lectures on Botany.* Author's collection.

PAGE 25: Emily Dickinson's herbarium, page 8: By permission of the Houghton Library, Harvard University (*MS AM 1118.9b Series II (79) & 84* and *MS Am 1118.11*).

PAGE 48: Emily Dickinson's herbarium, page 12: By permission of the Houghton Library, Harvard University (*MS AM 1118.9b Series II (79) & 84* and *MS Am 1118.11*).

PAGE 56: Horticultural Hall: By permission of the Massachusetts Horticultural Society.

PAGE 76: From the author's collection.

PAGE 85: From the author's collection.

PAGE 92: Emily Dickinson's conservatory: Courtesy of the Jones Library, Inc., Amherst, Mass.

PAGE 98: Lavinia Dickinson with one of her cats. Courtesy of the Jones Library, Inc., Amherst, Mass.

PAGE 101: The Evergreens, ca. 1920: Courtesy of the Jones Library, Inc., Amherst, Mass.

PAGE 118: Plate VI, Mrs. Almira H. Lincoln's *Familiar Lectures on Botany.* From the author's collection.

PAGE 134: A detail from a pictorial map of Amherst, Burleigh Lithographers, Troy, New York, 1886: Courtesy of the Jones Library, Inc., Amherst, Mass.

PAGE 135: Downtown Amherst, 1840: Courtesy of the Jones Library, Inc., Amherst, Mass.

PAGE 166: Looking east on Main Street: By permission of the Houghton Library, Harvard University (*MS AM 1118.9b Series II (79) & 84* and *MS Am 1118.11*).

PAGE 168: The Dickinson Homestead in winter: By permission of the Houghton Library, Harvard University (*MS AM 1118.9b Series II (79) & 84* and *MS Am 1118.11*).

PAGE 173: A panel with Indian pipes that Mabel Loomis Todd painted for Emily Dickinson and the first edition of Emily Dickinson's poems: Courtesy of the Folger Shakespeare Library, Washington, D.C., and the Amherst College Archives and Special Collections. By permission of the Trustees of Amherst College.

PAGE 181: The Bliss Catalogue: By permission of the Massachusetts Horticultural Society.

PAGE 193: Homestead garden photograph: the author.

INDEX